Faith alone is certainty. Everything but faith is subject to doubt. Jesus Christ alone is the certainty of faith.

Dietrich Bonhoeffer, *Ethics*

Proper Confidence

Faith, Doubt, and Certainty
in Christian Discipleship

LESSLIE NEWBIGIN

William B. Eerdmans Publishing Company
Grand Rapids, Michigan / Cambridge, U.K.

Published in 1995 by

Wm. B. Eerdmans Publishing Co.

2140 Oak Industrial Drive N.E., Grand Rapids, Michigan 49505 /

P.O. Box 163, Cambridge CB3 9PU U.K.

Printed in the United States of America

11 10 09 08 07 06   10 9 8 7 6 5

Library of Congress Cataloging-in-Publication Data

ISBN-10: 0-8028-0856-5

ISBN-13: 978-0-8028-0856-1

www.eerdmans.com

Contents

1

Faith as the Way to Knowledge

Anyone who attends to the discussions, debates, and controversies among Christians in this last decade of the second millennium is familiar with the issue I wish to address in this short essay. The words "liberal" and "fundamentalist" are used today not so much to identify oneself as to label the enemy. From one side comes the accusation that the mind of the fundamentalist is closed, shuttered against the possibility of doubt and therefore against the recognition of hitherto unrecognized truth. From the other side comes the charge that liberals are so open to new ideas that they have no firm commitments at all, that every affirmation of faith must be held only tentatively, and that every dogma must, as a matter of principle, be challenged. There are terms of moral opprobrium that each side employs to attack the other: the fundamentalist is arrogant, blinkered, and culturally illiterate; the liberal is flabby, timid, and carried along by every new fashion of thought. From the point of view of the fundamentalist, doubt is sin; from the point of view of the liberal, the capacity for doubt is a measure of intellectual integrity and honesty.

In addition to ascribing these accusations, labels, and genuine differences over doubt to both sides in this quarrel, it is also right to ascribe moral virtues to them: Liberalism at its best is marked by an open mind which is humble and ready to learn. Fundamentalism at its best is marked by a moral courage which holds fast to the truth even when it is assailed by counterclaims from without. In the currently prevailing atmosphere of relativism, where one does not speak of "what is true" but rather of what is "meaningful for me"; where one does not speak of right and wrong but of values; it is right and proper that there should be protest, and it is natural that this should lead to demands for absolute standards and certain truth. When everything in religion seems to be reduced to subjective experience, it is natural that there should be a demand for the affirmation of objective truth. Yet how can this affirmation be made without falling into the opposite error of arrogance, obscurantism, and fundamentalism? How can we develop, in respect of religious belief, minds which are not only open to fresh insights but also equipped with the critical faculty that can distinguish sense from nonsense and reality from illusion? What kind of confidence is proper for those who witness to the truth of the gospel?

How is this quarrel to be settled or at least converted into a constructive dialogue? One way is to look at its deep roots in the intellectual history of Europe. In order to understand the debate, we must remind ourselves of the two streams of history that have flowed into the life of Europe during the past two millennia. Briefly stated, they are the stream flowing from the philosophy of classical antiquity with its fountainhead in the histories of Greece and Rome, and the stream that comes from the history of Israel mediated through the Bible and the living memory of this history in the life of the Christian church.

We think of Europe as a distinct cultural entity, and indeed it is. If we look at a global map, however, it is obvious that Europe is only the western end of Asia. For uncounted millennia, Europe was the cul-de-sac into which wave after wave of migrants from Asia moved, each driving its predecessor farther into

2

the western peninsulas and islands where the ocean blocked any further movement west. If, as I have done, one takes a slow journey from southern India to western Europe, picking up the traces of Alexander's deep penetration into Asia and crossing the battlefield where the Persian Empire met, and sometimes defeated, the armies of Greece and Rome; one is vividly reminded that, until the rise of Arab power drove a thick wedge between Europe and Asia, the two were but parts of one living space. What has made Europe a distinct cultural and spiritual entity is the fact that, for a thousand years, the barbarian tribes who had found their home there were schooled in both the biblical story and the learning of classical antiquity, the legacy of Greece and Rome. These tribes, or at least their intellectual leaders, were taught to think in Greek and Latin, but the story that shaped their thinking was the Bible. Therefore, from the beginning of what we now call "Europe," there was a tension between historical and philosophical streams, one flowing from Greece and Rome and the other from Israel.

The Greeks, of course, knew about gods and about what were supposed to be divine revelations. The great thinkers who shaped the classical worldview of Greece and Rome did not regard these as the way by which one might come to know the ultimate nature of things. Divine revelation and knowledge of the gods were proper, perhaps, for an immature stage of human development, but reliable truth would ultimately be reached by other means. For Greek rationality, whether in its Platonic or its Aristotelian forms, the biblical story could not be the place where ultimate truth was to be found. The Jews, whose synagogues were in every major city, were a people apart. One could admire their high moral standards and perhaps their noble monotheism, but their religion was outside the main currents of philosophical investigation.

Christianity presented itself to the classical world as a development of this Jewish faith, but — unlike Judaism — it reached out in vigorous propaganda among all sectors of the people. Its scriptures were also offered in Greek, but more significantly, commentary and interpretation were available in Greek, not the Aramaic of the emerging rabbinic tradition. If the message of the gospel was to capture the cultural leadership of the classical world, there would have to be a diligent intellectual effort to relate the biblical story to the world of classical thought, a world whose medium was the Greek language, the language the church used in its own preaching. But how could the biblical message be communicated with the world of classical thought without being absorbed into and neutralized by that world of thought? At the heart of the Christian message was a new fact: God had acted — and let us remember that the original meaning of "fact" is the Latin *factum*, "something done." God had acted in a way that, if believed, must henceforth determine all our ways of thinking. It could not merely fit into existing ways of understanding the world without fundamentally changing them. According to Athanasius, it provided a new *arche*, a new starting point for all human understanding of the world. It could not form part of any worldview except one of which it was the basis, but at the same time it could only be communicated to the world of classical thought by using the language of classical thought.

Already in the New Testament we can see the beginning of the struggle to bridge this communication gap, to communicate Christianity's new and revolutionary fact in ways that could be grasped in the thought forms of classical culture and yet to prevent the biblical message from being absorbed and neutralized by them. The writer of the Fourth Gospel begins by introducing the word *logos,* a word familiar to readers in the world of the eastern Mediterranean, whether Greek or Hebrew. For the former, it referred to the ultimate impersonal entity which was at the heart of all coherence in the cosmos. An Indian analogy would be the word *dharma.* For the latter, it referred to the word of the living, personal Lord by which he had created the cosmos and continues to sustain it. Here contact is made with the reader. It is a familiar word, and we know roughly what it means. Immediately, however, the writer uses words which surely threaten to break off all contact: "The Word became flesh." The *logos* is identified with a man named Jesus whose story the writer is about to tell.

The reader now has two possibilities. He can shut the book. The writer is apparently talking nonsense. There is no way within the thought-world of either a Greek or a Jew in which the *logos* could be identified with a particular human being, certainly not with a human being who reportedly had been executed as a criminal. As long as the accepted patterns of Greek and Jewish thought continue in place, this writing makes no possible sense.

The other possibility is to read on, to listen to those who tell the story, and perhaps (indeed above all) to witness the cruel death of those who would rather face the lions in the circus than disavow this belief. If that course is pursued, then the very meaning of the word *logos* and the whole edifice of thought of which it is the keystone have to be taken down and rebuilt on this new foundation, this new *arche*. The language of Scripture, the evangelist announces, will be either the cornerstone or the stone of stumbling; it cannot be merely one of the building blocks in the whole structure of thought. There is, in other words, an intellectual analogy to those words of Jesus which were so scandalous to their first hearers: "Destroy this temple, and I will raise it again in three days" (John 2:19).

The implications of this radically new starting point for thought needed time to be grasped, especially when the edifice was as large and strong as that of classical thought. It involved a struggle which continued for several centuries. Some, like Tertullian, saw no possibility of accommodation between the two: "What has Jerusalem in common with Athens?" he asked, assuming the answer "Nothing." Others, like Origen of Alexandria, a scholar and profound student both of the Bible and of classical thought, sought to find the greatest possible common ground. Crucial to this struggle was the battle that Athanasius fought against the most powerful forces in the church to safeguard affirmation of the Incarnation as not simply a likeness of God but the very being of God himself. If that had not been secured, Christianity would have gradually disappeared, absorbed into the general mix of pagan religiosity in which we are free to construct our own images of God. In Chesterton's apt phrase, "Christianity would have gone to pot."

This new starting point, the new *arche,* required a radically new way of thinking about God. To begin with, if the *logos* had become part of history in this man Jesus, then two dualisms which were fundamental to classical thought were no longer tenable. One was the dualism between the "sensible" and the "intelligible," or — as we might say — between the material and the mental or spiritual. The other was the dualism between being and becoming. Obviously these two dualisms are closely related. So long as they form part of one's mental framework, it is simply impossible to believe that the God who is, in Tillich's phrase, "Being in Itself," should actually be part of terrestrial history — "crucified under Pontius Pilate." Yet this is precisely what the Fourth Gospel seeks, above all, to emphasize in point after point, that in this precisely dated historical happening for which various witnesses are available, the eternal being of God was actually present. Either one rejects this as absurd, or one's whole understanding of what the word "God" refers to has to be reconsidered. The starting point for this reconsideration could not be found in any supposedly immutable principles of thought; it had to be found in the actual story the apostolic witnesses had told from the beginning.

It took many generations to hammer out a new understanding of God, and it is not surprising that there were often fierce disagreements along the way. After all, what can be more important for human life than to know who God is? The result of these generations of struggle was, as we know, the gradual clarification of a new way of understanding God as Father, Son, and Holy Spirit who, in their eternal mutuality of love, constitute what we mean by the word "God."

In his brilliant study *Christianity and Classical Culture,* Charles Norris Cochrane shows how this new paradigm overcame the dualisms that were paralyzing the classical world. It provided the starting point for a whole new chapter in human thought and action, a new beginning which was destined to shape what we now call Europe. Ultimate reality was no longer unknowable: it was available to us in the person of Jesus Christ, who was made known to us in the New Testament and the preaching of the church. By faithfulness to this reality, we would be led by the work of the divine Spirit to full knowledge of the Father, a knowledge partial here *in via* but promised in its fullness at the end.

Of special significance for the subsequent development of Europe is the work done during the latter part of the fourth century by Christian theologians in discussion with the science of their day. Christopher Kaiser, in his book *Creation and the History of Science,* has shown how the Cappadocian theologians developed four fundamental principles that were to shape the development of science through the centuries and up to the present day. The important point to note here is that these principles were formulated on the basis of belief in the divine revelation given in Scripture and supremely in the work of Christ. In brief, these principles were as follows:

1. Because the cosmos is the creation of a rational God who has also made us in his image, it follows that the cosmos is in principle comprehensible by the human mind. It is a coherent cosmos, not a chaos of random events. Therefore, (in contrast to important strands in Indian thought) there are no ultimate self-contradictions. It is not to be understood in terms of a yin-yang duality as in Far Eastern thought. It has an ultimate coherence, a coherence of which the central secret is made known in the Incarnation.

2. Because the cosmos is a creation by God as a free act of his will and not an emanation of God (as in some elements in Indian thought), the cosmos has a relative autonomy. Not everything that happens is the direct will of God. It follows, then, that the way to knowledge of the cosmos is not opening the mind to ultimate reality through mystical contemplation. To discover how the cosmos works, we must investigate the empirical facts by careful observation.

3. Because Scripture says that God created the heavens and the earth, it follows that the "heavenly bodies" are not (as Aristotle said) made of a substance different from the elements that comprise the earth, but are, on the contrary, of the same substance. (It is one of the many ironies in the history of the later conflicts between science and religion that when Galileo, as a result of his use of a telescope, decided that the moon was made of the same substance as the earth, he was condemned by the church because the church had meanwhile co-opted Aristotelian philosophy into its doctrine.)

4. Because of the work of Christ in the incarnation, we may use material means for the advancement of human salvation. The implication of this was that the church did not have to follow the Hebrew tradition of rejecting Greek medicine; instead, it could use Greek medicine in the development of the healing ministry which was to be such an important part of its work in succeeding centuries.

These four principles, which were to provide the foundation for the subsequent development of science in Europe (a science which was destined to outstrip the far more brilliant thinking of India, China, and the Arab world), were based on faith in the biblical revelation. They were part of the whole reconstitution of thought necessitated by the new fact, the action of God, the incarnation of the Word in Jesus Christ.

The work of the theologians of the first four centuries laid the foundation for a new way of understanding the world. As we shall be reminded many times, it did not mean the end of the tension between the classical and the biblical ways of understanding. It did ensure, however, that for nearly a thousand years it was the biblical story which was to have the greater part in shaping the thought of Europe. A crucial figure as far as Western Europe is concerned is Augustine of Hippo (354–430). Augustine was a brilliant product of the classical world. He was a master of the finest classical thought, although sadly he apparently never learned Greek, and, for various reasons, the Eastern Orthodox churches never venerated him as the West has done. He was professor of rhetoric in the imperial university and a supreme master in that field, as anyone who reads him today will acknowledge. But when, through the influence of Ambrose and through the circumstances of his own moral and intellectual struggles, he was brought to faith in Christ, he became an apprentice in the tradition which had its center in the biblical story. He took the biblical story as the starting point for a way of understanding which required a radical reconstruction of his former ways of thought. In his famous slogan *credo ut intelligam* (I believe in order to know), he defined a way of knowing that begins with the faithful acceptance of the given fact that God revealed himself in Christ.

Clearly, much of the mental furniture that Augustine had acquired through his long apprenticeship in the classical world of thought remains in his Christian writings. But there is a radically new starting point. The dominant element in his classical background is Platonic. For Plato, the ultimate realities were ideas, which are more or less fully realized in the various entities which are the objects of our experience. It is by grasping these eternal ideas and participating in them that the soul attains its true being and its salvation. These ideas constitute a hierarchy of which the Idea of the Good is the apex. The other major

9

strand of classical thought, that strand which originates in Plato's great disciple Aristotle, is more concerned with the causal relations among things in the world of becoming. As we shall see, this Aristotelian tradition was to play a major role in the development of Europe at a later stage.

What is obvious and important at this stage is that the acceptance of the biblical tradition as a starting point for thought constituted a radical break with the classical tradition, whether in its Platonic or Aristotelian form. To put it crudely, in the latter form we begin by asking questions, and we formulate these questions on the basis of our experience of the world. In this enterprise we are in control of operations. We decide which questions to ask, and these decisions necessarily condition the nature of the answers. This is the procedure with which we are familiar in the work of the natural sciences. The things we desire to understand are not active players in the game of learning; they are inert and must submit to our questioning. The resulting "knowledge" is our achievement and our possession.

But there is another kind of knowing which, in many languages, is designated by a different word. It is the kind of knowing that we seek in our relations with other people. In this kind of knowing we are not in full control. We may ask questions, but we must also answer the questions put by the other. We can only come to know others in the measure in which they are willing to share. The resulting knowledge is not simply our own achievement; it is also the gift of others. And even in the mutual relations of ordinary human beings, it is never complete. There are always further depths of knowledge that only long friendship and mutual trust can reach, if indeed they can be reached at all.

There is a radical break between these two kinds of knowing: the knowing often associated with the natural sciences and the knowing involved in personal relations. We experience this radical break, for example, when someone about whom we have been talking unexpectedly comes into the room. We can discuss an absent person in a manner that leaves us in full control of the discussion. But if the person comes into the room, we must either break off the discussion or change into a different mode of talking.

This is a proper analogy of the break involved in the move from the classical to the Christian way of understanding the world. If, so to say, the Idea of the Good has actually entered the room and spoken, we have to stop our former discussion and listen. Instead of asking all the questions, we must answer the questions put by the Other. Of course it is possible to dismiss the interruption. The one who has entered the room may be an impostor, and we can treat this possible imposter with skepticism, declining to accept the claimed identity. That is always a possibility. But if we recognize the intruder as the one we were talking about, then one kind of talk has to stop and another has to begin.

Is there, then, a total discontinuity between the classical and the Christian ways of understanding? Was Tertullian right? The answer is both "yes" and "no." There is indeed the discontinuity of which I have spoken. But there is also a continuity in the sense that by listening to the intruder we shall find in the end that we have found better answers to our questions than before, when apart from the intruder we formulated our own questions. This might be dismissed as a rash and unprovable assertion. At this point in my essay, I would only defend it by referring again to the story of Western science. Science has developed in Europe in a way that has far outstripped the work of ancient Greek, Egyptian, and Indian science because it was willing to take as its starting point affirmations rooted in the biblical revelation of God as creator and redeemer. Questioning can go on forever and lead nowhere. There are always fresh questions which can be asked. Asking questions can become an all-consuming passion which can never be satisfied, for which any claim to know the truth is a kind of treason against the intellect. A recent writer has wittily suggested that there is a parallel between this certain kind of academic tradition and the tradition of fox-hunting. The whole point is the chase; if the fox is actually caught, the fun is all over, and we have to look for another fox. Surely, the asking of questions is a vital part of our encounter with reality. But reality finally encounters us when we have to answer the question put to us by the incarnate *logos*: "Who do you say that I am?" Similarly, one hopes that one day the hunter is confronted with the cruel reality of hounding a fox to death.

Augustine lived, thought, and wrote while the classical world was crumbling around him and Rome, the eternal city, was being sacked by the barbarians. In one of the greatest writings of humankind, his *Confessions,* he tells the story of how he sought and did not find, but was found by the one he sought. From then on there was a new starting point for his questing and questioning. The story of God's mighty acts in the creation and redemption of the world through the Word made flesh in the actual history of Jesus Christ, not a belief in the Idea of Good, would henceforth be the foundation for all the great intellectual and spiritual striving which filled the remaining years of his life.

And it was this same biblical story that was to shape the life of Europe for the ensuing period of nearly a thousand years. What we now call Europe was, during Augustine's life, a medley of barbarian tribes and petty kingdoms, all making their claims to sovereignty in the midst of the dead and dying remnants of the old Roman imperial order. There was no coherent political structure or common intellectual and spiritual coherence.

Still, it was the Christian church that alone could offer the foundation for a new order. In doing so, it certainly had the advantage that it carried with it much of the prestige of the former empire. That Roman civilization had been an affair of cities: the tribes who had taken over Europe were not city dwellers. The church had developed in its Mediterranean heartland primarily in the cities. In addition, it now found a new and powerful means of penetration into a rural society. The monastic movement had arisen in the East as a protest against the growing worldliness of the urban Christianity that flourished after Constantine. St. Benedict was the greatest of those in the West who took over, but profoundly modified, this Eastern monastic tradition in order to create a growing network of monastic communities which would eventually cover the whole of Western Europe. The Benedictine rule, with its balanced combination of prayer, manual work, and study, was firmly based on the Bible. At the center of the life of each community was the continual reading of the Bible, both in study and in the worship of the community. The biblical story came to be the one story that shaped the understanding of who we are, where we come from, and where we are going. In the constant remembering of the great events of creation and salvation through the liturgical year, in the popular drama of the streets, and in the pictures that surrounded the congregation as they gathered for worship, it was this story that was their mental framework, the story that defined human life and its meaning and destiny. It was this story that shaped those barbarian tribes into the cultural and spiritual entity that made Europe something other than simply a peninsula of Asia. And because Europe later developed that way of thinking and organizing life which is now known throughout the world as "modernity," we cannot understand modernity without understanding this part of our history.

I have spoken of the radical character of the switch from the classical worldview to that which was based on the biblical story. Needless to say, there is no way of demonstrating that the one is superior to the other. There is a fundamental difference between a worldview which sees ultimate reality as in some sense personal, therefore to be known only in the way that we can have knowledge of another person, and the worldview which sees ultimate reality as impersonal — as (for example) does the Indian tradition. There is no principle more fundamental than either of these views and by which one could, therefore, adjudicate between them. Personal knowledge is impossible without risk; it cannot begin without an act of trust, and trust can be betrayed. We are here facing a fundamental decision in which we have to risk everything we have. There are no insurance policies available.

It may be helpful, however, to spell out two ways in which these radically different ways of understanding diverge:

1. If the place where we look for ultimate truth is in a story and if (as is the case) we are still in the middle of the story, then it follows that we walk by faith and not by sight. If ultimate truth is sought in an idea, a formula, or a set of timeless laws or principles, then we do not have to recognize the possibility that something totally unexpected may happen. Insofar as our knowledge is accurate, we shall be able to predict the future. Future and past are governed by the same laws, the same principles, and the same realities. But if we find ultimate truth in a story that has not yet been finished, we do not have that kind of certainty. The certainty we have rests on the faithfulness of the one whose story it is. We walk by faith.

2. The two worldviews differ in respect to the roles of seeing and hearing. In the classical view, the true knowledge is vision, *theoria*. It is the vision of eternal truth. One therefore makes a distinction between *theoria* and *praxis*. One must first grasp the vision and then, in a second step, find ways of embodying it in action. Readers of the Bible will have noticed that these terms are totally absent. Because ultimate reality is personal, God's address to us is a word conveying his purpose and promise, a word which may be heard or ignored, obeyed or disobeyed. Faith comes by hearing, and unbelief is disobedience. In the words of Dietrich Bonhoeffer, "Only the obedient believe, and those who believe are obedient" (*The Cost of Discipleship*, p. 69). As we shall see, the replacement of this biblical distinction between faith and unbelief with the classical distinction between theory and practice has had momentous results.

2

Doubt as the Way to Certainty

The centuries following the death of Augustine are often spoken of as the Dark Ages. They were a time when, outwardly at least, events were dominated by the newly established barbarian kingdoms. But throughout this period the influence of Christianity was permeating society, above all through the work of the Benedictine monastic communities. In contrast to the eastern half of the old empire, where the Greek inheritance was most powerful, in Western Christendom the Latin tradition had the greatest influence. Greek thought, insofar as it was present, was mainly in its Platonic form.

Meanwhile, Aristotelian philosophy had found a new home. Western Christians often forget that, in the earliest centuries of the church, some of its greatest advances took place in the region which Europeans call the Middle East and which Indians call West Asia. Here the language of Christian literature was not Greek but Syriac. The "Church of the East," with its great center at Edessa, became a point from which Christianity radiated to places as far as Persia, Afghanistan, India, and China. The Christians of the "Church of the East" had already translated Aristotle into Syriac when the great explosion of Arab power, inspired by the message of Islam, overwhelmed the Christian civilization of

16

the region. These "Nestorian" Christians eventually became the teachers of their Arab overlords; in due course, Aristotle was translated into Arabic, and Islamic theology took Aristotelian rationalism into its heart. While Western Europe was still coming out of its Dark Ages, Islam had become a very rich culture, much more advanced in the arts of civilization than Western Christendom. It was especially in Spain in the eleventh and twelfth centuries that there was much mutual contact between theologians of Islamic, Jewish and Christian traditions, and it was here that Aristotle was translated into Latin. Above all, it was the translation into Latin of the writings of the great Muslim theologians, such as Avicenna (980–1032) and Averroes (1126–1198), that brought into the thinking of Western Christendom a new kind of rationalism that challenged the traditional ways of thought.

How was the challenge to be met? The popularity in the University of Paris of Averroes' teachings led the Pope in 1263 to reimpose an earlier ban on the teaching of Aristotle, but "The Philosopher," as Aristotle was often called, could not be silenced. Already in 1257 St. Thomas Aquinas (c. 1225–74) had begun his *Summa contra Gentiles,* and it was Thomas who was to achieve a synthesis of the new learning with the old biblical tradition, a synthesis which was to shape the thinking of Western Christendom to this day.

Averroism was making deep inroads into Christian thought. It made a sharp distinction between faith and reason and taught a doctrine of "double truth" which allowed the believer to hold doctrines that a philosopher had to deny. In attacking this false teaching, Thomas accepted a distinction between things that can be known by reason alone (such as the existence of God and the immortality of the soul) and things that could be known only by faith through divine revelation, such as the doctrines of the Incarnation and the Trinity. Thomas argued against Averroes, however, that where divine revelation contradicts the findings

17

of philosophy, the latter are untrue, or can be shown to be unnecessary. Theology was therefore a higher discipline than philosophy. But reason and faith had been pried apart, and the Thomistic tradition, which was to shape the thought of Western Christendom for many centuries, did not always follow the careful distinctions made by Thomas. In particular, it became common to regard philosophy as the necessary prolegomena to theology; the findings of theology had to be validated by philosophy. Three consequences of this are important for the present discussion.

1. The Thomist scheme puts asunder what Augustine had held together, and as a result of this, knowledge is separated from faith. There is a kind of knowledge for which one does not have to depend on faith, and there is another kind which is only available by the exercise of faith. It does not need to be pointed out that this dichotomy has run deep in our culture to this day. Certain knowledge is one thing; faith is something else. In Locke's famous definition, belief is "a persuasion which falls short of knowledge." Certainty is a matter of knowledge, not of faith. Faith is what we have to fall back on when certain knowledge is not to be had. Here one can see the origins of that split which runs right through contemporary Western thought, the split which gives rise to what C. P. Snow called "The Two Cultures" and which runs through every university campus separating the buildings devoted to science from those devoted to other pursuits.

2. The second consequence of this move is to create a cleavage between two conceptions of God. The God whose existence is demonstrable by the methods of philosophical argument is not easily recognizable as the God who encounters us in the Bible. He is certainly not the Trinity of Christian faith. It is almost impossible to conceive that this God could become incarnate in a particular human being. One is faced with a dilemma: Which is the real God? Is the God of the philosophers

the real God, and thus the God who encounters us in the biblical story perhaps a primitive anthropomorphic misunderstanding, appropriate to an early stage in human development but to be left behind in a more developed society? Or is the true and living God the one who meets us in the Bible, the one who meets us in the person of Jesus Christ? If this is the case, is the God of the philosophers a construct of the human mind, a work not of men's hands but of their minds, an idol? It is obvious that this dilemma has remained at the heart of Christian thinking in the "developed" world to this day.

3. The third consequence of the Thomist synthesis is perhaps the most far-reaching of all. If philosophy has to be called in to underpin that knowledge of God which (it is claimed) comes by revelation; if, in other words, the religious experience of those apprenticed to the tradition which has its foundation in the biblical narrative is not in itself a sufficient ground for certainty, so that other, more reliable grounds are to be sought; it follows that those other grounds must be completely reliable. The philosophical proofs for the existence of God must be invulnerable. But they are not. The centuries following St. Thomas saw the increasing influence of classical thought at the time of the Renaissance and — above all — the shaking of old and (apparently) secure foundations by the findings of the new science as developed by Galileo, Copernicus, and Kepler. All of this added to the weight of skepticism. If seemingly age-old certainties were now called into question, where could certainty be found? That the sun rose in the east and went down in the west had seemed, since the dawn of human consciousness, one of the most certain facts of human experience. But in the centuries following St. Thomas and up to today, we have been asked to believe that this is not so, but that it is the earth which moves — despite the fact that it seems as solid as ever.

By the beginning of the seventeenth century, skepticism was dominant in the intellectual life of Western Europe. According to Michael Buckley (*At the Origins of Modern Atheism,* 1987), the question asked throughout France was, Is there any escape from skepticism? This was not primarily a matter of belief in God but of whether or not any reliable knowledge whatsoever was possible. Indeed, this kind of skepticism could go along with a certain kind of theism, for the abstractly omnipotent "God" of natural theology was above the jurisdiction of human logic. But outright atheism was "knocking at the door." It was in this intellectual atmosphere that a famous debate took place at a Paris conference in November 1628. At this conference, a learned philosopher undertook to show that skepticism could be overcome by recognizing the force of probability and that probability, in turn, could be accepted as a sufficient basis for knowledge. At this meeting was a young philosopher named René Descartes. The enthusiasm with which the audience acclaimed this defense of probability roused his ire, and he intervened, proceeding to demonstrate that on the basis of probability he could prove truth to be falsehood and falsehood to be truth. Philosophy could not be content with probability, and by Descartes's method, certain knowledge was within reach.

Also present at the conference was the Cardinal Pierre de Bérulle (1575–1629), who was deeply impressed by Descartes's intervention. The subject of the discussion at the conference was not the existence of God but the possibility of escaping from skepticism. The cardinal was concerned about the threat of atheism. The upshot of his conversation with Descartes was that Descartes received from the cardinal a commission to deploy his philosophical method to prove, beyond doubt, the existence of God. In this commission two goals were put together: the defeat of skepticism and the defeat of atheism. "Never," remarks Buckley, "were two adversaries more fatally merged into one" (*Origins,* p. 72).

Descartes's method involved an initial alliance with the skeptics. He would clear the ground of everything, that is, everything that was not certain, everything that was a matter of faith but not a matter of knowledge. Having cleared the ground of unreliable materials he would lay a foundation "which was self-justifying and self-authenticating, principles so intuitive that they admitted no denial and were even sustained by the exercise of doubt" (*Origins,* p. 72). He affirmed that the knowledge of God and of the soul was the business of philosophy, not of theology. Natural reason alone can provide certain knowledge. As is well known, Descartes found the self-justifying intuition on which to build the new edifice of certain knowledge in his own existence as a thinking subject. Thus even skepticism is made to serve the cause of knowledge, for one's skepticism is evidence of one's existence as a thinking (and doubting) subject. From this indubitable starting point, Descartes set out to build the structure of knowledge by processes of reasoning which had the clarity and indubitability of mathematics. A mathematical equation, once it is understood, cannot be doubted. Mathematics was, in fact, to become the *lingua franca* of all the varied branches of scientific knowledge which were to develop as the method of Descartes came to be applied in all fields of inquiry. (It is perhaps worth mentioning here that this is another vital point at which the development of Western European thought has been determined by a contribution from the house of Islam, for one cannot imagine modern mathematics ever developing if the old Roman numerals had not been replaced by the Arabic ones.)

One can see that Descartes was building his new structure of indubitable knowledge on the foundation of skepticism, the skepticism that was the dominant intellectual climate of his time. He was thus reversing the method of Augustine. Doubt, not faith, was to be the path to knowledge. By relentless skepticism, the famous "critical principles," every claim to truth was to be put through the critical sieve in which only the indubitable would be retained. This was the body of knowledge. The rest was belief, faith, or at most probability.

This method of Descartes would dominate the development of thought in Europe for three centuries, and no one can question the magnitude of what has been achieved by its employment. We are now living, however, in a period when Descartes's method is widely criticized and abandoned. Before looking at the way in which this disillusionment has occurred, it is useful to draw attention to three major consequences of Descartes's move. In the first place, it strongly reinforced the dualism of mind and matter which had been such a debilitating feature of the classical world-view. By isolating the thinking mind as though it existed apart from its embodiment in a whole person and thus apart from the whole human and cosmic history to which that person belongs, Descartes opened a huge gap between the world of thought and the world of material things and historical happenings. In his method, the gap was bridged by means of a multi-step argument: from the doubting and therefore fallible human mind one argues the existence of a perfect mind which knows no doubt or fallibility; the existence of this perfect mind ("God") assures us that our senses will not be allowed to deceive us and that we can therefore know that the material world exists. But this complex argument does not overcome the dualism that has been a mark of European thought in the past three centuries: the mental (or spiritual) and the material are two separate worlds.

The second consequence, related to the first but worthy of separate mention, is the divorce between the objective and the subjective poles in human knowing and the consequent polarization between objectivity and subjectivity. This has led, in turn, to a popular image of science as a realm of objective facts which are quite sanitized of any elements of subjectivity, with the corollary that all other claims to knowledge — for instance, claims in the realms of art, literature, poetry, and religion — are merely subjective. The best scientists in all times, and recent scientific work in particular, have totally repudiated this image, but it was used by men like Huxley in the nineteenth century to propagate the myth that science had replaced religion as the centerpiece of modern civilization. This myth is still powerful today.

The third effect of the Cartesian program has been to reinforce the dichotomy, already referred to, between theory and practice. Things would have been different if Descartes had taken as his starting point "I act, therefore I am," or "I love, therefore I am." But Descartes wanted absolute certainty. One could be mistaken about acting and loving. But thinking, even if it is wrong thinking, necessarily presupposes a thinker. His own existence as a thinker gave Descartes the indubitable certainty that he required. By isolating the thinking mind, detaching it from the world of acting and loving, Descartes reintroduced this classical dichotomy. Thinking out the principles is one thing; putting them into practice is another step. The results of this are such as to justify the protest of those who want to reverse the order and put practice before theory. But this is no solution. It only means that we act on assumptions which we have not examined.

Despite its immense effects on the subsequent history of Europe, the Cartesian program has run into difficulties. The fundamental reason can be stated simply: the centerpiece of Descartes's method is the critical principle. Every truth claim must be open to criticism. Doubt is to be applied to all beliefs, however ancient and venerable, and only those that prove to be indubitable can be accepted. One may distinguish three forms in which doubt can be expressed.

1. If you make the assertion "I believe P," I may say "I doubt P because I believe Q, R, and T," which are incompatible with P. In other words, my doubt rests upon a faith commitment. It is, of course, possible to doubt Q, R, and T but, once again, only on the basis of other beliefs which I do not doubt, at least not at the moment of doubting Q, R, and T. This form of doubt, therefore, presupposes faith.

2. I may say, "I doubt P because you have not proved it."

This implies that there are criteria of proof by which P could be either proved or disproved. But the existence of these criteria is also open to doubt. I cannot offer this form of agnostic doubt unless I offer it on the basis of a set of beliefs (about the validity of these criteria) which — for the moment — I do not doubt.

3. There is also, of course, total skepticism, doubting that it is possible to make any truth claims at all. This total skepticism is indeed a possibility, as illustrated in the Europe of the seventeenth century and in the Europe of today. What is to be said about this? Quite simply, it is an intellectual pose and not a genuine belief. So long as we continue to live we continually act on the assumption that certain things are true and others not. To live we must eat, and to eat we must believe that the food set before us will nourish and not poison us. The only logical implication of total skepticism would be suicide. This logical conclusion is rarely (but, alas, sometimes) drawn by individuals. But if total skepticism becomes the intellectual fashion of a whole society, then that society is quite certainly on the road to its demise.

By the mercy of God, human beings are often saved from their intellectual follies, and so European society has not yet perished. But the method of Descartes has cast a deep shadow of skepticism over the subsequent history of European thought, even in the midst of the superb technical achievements it has made possible. At the most obvious level it has created a prejudice in favor of doubt over faith. The phrases "blind faith" and "honest doubt" have become the most common of currency. Both faith and doubt can be honest or blind, but one does not hear of "blind doubt" or of "honest faith." Yet the fashion of thought which gives priority to doubt over faith in the whole adventure of knowing is absurd. Both faith and doubt are necessary elements in this adventure. One does not learn anything except by believing something, and — conversely — if one doubts everything one learns nothing. On the other hand, believing everything uncritically is the road to disaster. The faculty of doubt is essential. But as I have argued, rational doubt always rests on faith and not vice versa. The relation between the two cannot be reversed. Knowing always begins with the opening of our minds and our senses to the great reality which is around us and which sustains us, and it always depends on this from beginning to end. The capacity to doubt, to question what seems obvious, is a necessary element in our effort to know reality as it is, but its role is derivative and secondary. Rational doubt depends on faith; rational faith does not depend on doubt.

Immanuel Kant (1724–1804) was perhaps the greatest thinker in the centuries following Descartes. In his most influential work, *Critique of Pure Reason,* he demonstrated the limits of reason, arguing that our reason alone cannot reach beyond the appearance of things (the phenomena) to the ultimate reality which lies, so to speak, behind them (the noumenon). In his two succeeding works, *Critique of Practical Reason* and *Critique of Judgment,* Kant sought to show how our moral experience and our aesthetic experience can lead us beyond the boundary that defines the limits of reason. He showed how our moral experience requires us to acknowledge the reality of God, of judgment, and of immortality.

Kant's was one of the most powerful minds ever engaged in wrestling with these issues, and the popular interpretations of his thinking have, almost inevitably, oversimplified his conclusions. Because the first of the three *Critiques* has received the greatest attention, its negative conclusion — that the existence of God is beyond the reach of human reason — has been among his most powerful legacies. That "ultimate reality is unknowable" has become almost a self-evident truth for "modern" people, who do not notice the self-contradictory character of this assertion: how does one know that something is unknowable? Kant's positive affirmations about the being of God rested primarily on the sense of the absolute character of the moral law. But the development of "modernity" since the Enlightenment, with its emphasis on reason as the only path to reliable knowledge, has weakened this sense of a moral absolute. Kant was the product of a devout Christian home where the commandments of God were the basis of the moral law. His argument from the fact of moral obligation to the existence of God, however, has not been followed in succeeding generations. Rather, the reasoning has been that since there is no God, there is no moral law. Kant was seeking to establish room for faith in a society threatened by skeptical rationalism. Sadly, the positive thrust of his reasoning was lost in the popular understanding of his work.

It was Friederich Nietzsche (1844–1900) who, at the end of the nineteenth century, drew with inescapable clarity the necessary conclusion of the method of Descartes. For the reason already given, the critical principle must necessarily destroy itself. Rational criticism rests on beliefs which are, for the moment, held acritically. But these beliefs are themselves liable to critical questioning. If the critical principle is exalted to the supreme place in the enterprise of knowing, then the possibility of knowing anything is destroyed. "True" and "false," "right" and "wrong" — these are now words which have no objective reference. They are simply expressions of the will. The will to power is the real driving force of history. The "eternal truths of reason" so beloved during the Age of Reason are in fact nothing of the kind; they are the products of particular historical developments and of particular exercises of the will to power. The twentieth century has learned this lesson. Claims to speak meaningfully about right and wrong are discounted. Instead, one speaks of "values." These "values" are a matter of personal choice. They express what the person who holds them wishes to see enacted. They are precisely expressions of the will (albeit in a less brutal form than that suggested by Nietzsche).

The age which accepted the method of Descartes for the attainment of reliable truth referred to itself as the Age of Reason.

It believed that by faithfulness to these methods one would attain to certainty and to reliable truth, in contrast to the traditional beliefs based on alleged revelation, which rested their claims on faith rather than on reason. In the last decades of this century, the intellectual leadership of Europe has begun to turn its back on modernity. We are in the age of postmodernity. The mark of this is a suspicion of all claims to universal truth. Such claims have to be deconstructed. The "metanarratives" told by societies to validate their claims to global power are to be rejected. There are no privileged cultures and no privileged histories. All human cultures are equally entitled to respect. There are only different "regimes of truth" (Michel Foucault) which succeed one another. Each one suppresses the claims of the previous one to know truth and imposes its own rule. There are no overarching criteria by which these regimes can be judged. The ultimate factor in history, as Nietzsche saw it, is the will to power. Violence is the fundamental element of human life and history.

The modern age began with the daring program of Descartes, a program encouraged by a cardinal of the church and designed to banish skepticism once and for all by establishing the method by which indubitable certainty could be obtained. Neither faith nor probability would suffice. Certainty was possible, and we ought to be content with nothing less. It is deeply ironic that this method has led us directly into the profound skepticism of the postmodern world. The greatest product of the modern age is the work of science, a work which has transformed the human situation and continues to do so. Yet there is now a profound skepticism about science itself. It is recognized as a unique avenue to power (and the greater part of scientific work is now directed towards the achievement of power — military, industrial, and commercial), but it is not perceived as a pathway to wisdom. Modern science has placed in human hands the power to do things that were previously unimaginable. Technology, the development of ever more sophisticated means for achieving any end we choose, dominates modern and modernized societies. But there is a growing perception that science and technology are no substitute for wisdom — for the power to discern what ends are in accordance with the truth and the power to judge rightly between alternative ends.

If it is true that the author and sustainer of all that exists is the God who has made himself known to us in Jesus Christ, then it is a simple truth that "the fear of the Lord is the beginning of wisdom." In spite of the role that the Supreme Being plays in Descartes's method, it did not take long for the critical principle to remove God from the realm of certain knowledge. Whatever his intentions, Descartes bequeathed to Europe a confidence that certain knowledge could be achieved without reference to God. The often quoted words of the astronomer Laplace, when questioned by Napoleon about the omission of God from his systematic worldview, truly express a point of view that dominated European thought until very recently: "I had no need of that hypothesis." That confidence has largely evaporated. The popularity of talk about spirituality and the growing influence of the complex of ideas expressed in the New Age movement, as well as the new eagerness to turn to the writings of Asian religion in search of wisdom, are all symptoms of this change. The idea that wisdom comes from the East is having a new lease on life.

But if the biblical story is true, the kind of certainty proper to a human being will be one which rests on the fidelity of God, not upon the competence of the human knower. It will be a kind of certainty which is inseparable from gratitude and trust.

28

3

Certainty as the Way to Nihilism

The seventeenth and eighteenth centuries saw a rapid development in the new science. Perhaps its supreme achievement was the mathematical physics of Isaac Newton. It is hard to exaggerate the impact that Newton's work made on the mind of Europe. It seemed that he had found the final answer to the question: "How does the cosmos really work?" His model seemed to provide a clue to the understanding of everything from the movement of the stars to the fall of an apple. Descartes's vision of a world ultimately understood in terms of the indubitable certainties of mathematics seemed to be vindicated. The whole universe could, it seemed, be understood with the clarity of mathematics. Alexander Pope's famous lines expressed what was widely felt among the intellectual leaders of Europe:

> Nature and Nature's laws lay hid in night;
> God said: "Let Newton be" and all was light.

Here was a model of reality that did not depend on divine revelation or on faith. It was a model that any cultivated intelligence could understand. Here was the possibility of liberation from the ancient tyrannies of religion and superstition. The heavy weight of ecclesiastical authority, backed by the threat of supernatural sanctions, need no longer terrify. Human reason, released from this bondage, could find the truth.

There was a further reason for a renunciation of the authority of religion. The seventeenth century saw the fabric of Western Christendom torn to pieces by the religious wars. For decades Christians soaked the soil of Europe with blood, warring over their rival interpretations of the Christian message. It is surely not surprising that this dazzling new vision of reality should have exerted such a powerful attraction. A new light was dawning, and a bloodstained past could be seen for what it was — the Dark Ages, or, as the light slowly began to penetrate, the Middle Ages, the period between the ancient glory of classical culture and the newly dawning age of reason. Skepticism about ultimate reality might not have been banished, but the new science opened up, to the immense benefit of the human race, a sufficiently exciting prospect of exploring the world of appearances.

By the middle of the eighteenth century, Europeans were speaking of their own age as the Age of Reason, the Enlightenment. And this new confidence had explosive power. Here was a new prospect for the whole human race. The light that had dawned in Europe now had to be spread throughout the world. The Dark Ages might have passed in Europe, but there were still dark continents where the light had not penetrated. Human reason was essentially the same everywhere, and all human beings, whatever their race or creed, could be taught to share the benefits of its unfettered use. Here was a task worthy of the supreme dedication of the peoples of Europe. Europe now had a mission to civilize the world.

First, however, Europe itself had to shake off its old chains. The French Revolution was the explosion awaking Europe to the fact that a force, unlike anything known in Europe's past, had been generated by the new way of thinking. The vision of liberation, of the right of every human being to justice and freedom, had to be translated into the realities of politics. "Liberty" and "equality" were the watchwords, with "fraternity" a somewhat muted third cry. France was the first place where the explosion took place, but the Napoleonic wars carried many of the new ideas into the rest of Europe. Nothing in Europe would ever be the same.

But this explosive force also triggered a reaction. In Germany, especially, but not exclusively, there was the reaction of the romantic movement. Mathematical reason could not do justice to the fullness of human experience. There are things in human life — art, music, architecture, ancient myths and sagas so full of another kind of wisdom, traditional ways of ordering social life — all of these were precious things which could not be exhaustively mapped on the grid of mathematics. This was the context in which the word *kultur* came into a new use, later to be transferred to England where the first use of the word "culture" in this sense occurs in 1867. "Culture" is, of course, originally concerned with such things as agriculture and horticulture. It now came to be used to speak of those things that a society holds in common and holds as precious for its continuing life as a community.

European culture (in this new sense) was sufficiently homogeneous for the rational and romantic elements to challenge each other in a way that was not destructive. A different situation arose when the explosive power of the Enlightenment drove Europeans to Asia, the Pacific Islands, and Africa, with each of these areas possessing cultures vastly different from Europe. Europeans had become aware of these widely differing cultures through reports by Jesuit missionaries from the early seventeenth century onward. These brought to the attention of Europe the existence of societies whose cultures were vastly different from that of Europe. But although the word "culture" came to be used in a sociological sense in the nineteenth century, it was not used

31

in the plural. There was one "civilization" and the various peoples encountered in other continents were on lower or higher rungs of this one ladder. They did not have different "cultures" (until the present century) but were considered either less or more civilized. It was the task of the European peoples to bring the blessings of civilization to the rest of the world.

Inevitably this triggered a reaction comparable to the one that had occurred in Europe, but now on a much greater scale and of a much more radical kind. The peoples invaded by European civilization were roused to a passionate defense of those elements of their traditional cultures which were ignored or devalued in the calculus of European rationalism. There was now something much more radical than the intra–European tension between the rationalist and romantic forces: there was a radical repudiation of Europe's claim to have a mission to civilize the world.

This reaction did not gather strength until the second half of the twentieth century, after the devastation of Europe in the two world wars. In the earlier period of European invasion, there was much in the Western package that was attractive, especially to the underprivileged members of the societies being invaded. And the reaction is still qualified by the fact that these societies, perceiving the benefits accruing from the use of modern technology, are generally eager to share in these benefits. This places them in a painful dilemma: how far is it possible to take on board the technology of the West and the science undergirding it without eroding and eventually destroying precious elements in the traditional culture? The very sharpness of this unresolved dilemma also gives a sharpness to the repudiation of Western cultural imperialism.

This strong counterattack against the values of the European Enlightenment has come just at the time when, for the reasons already given, the confidence of Europe in its own culture is collapsing. The result of the conjunction of these two

Moral obligation Standing for God
we image obligation

forces is the phenomenon of multiculturalism, an ideology that celebrates cultural diversity as an unqualified good in its own right. When this ideology takes over, value judgments claiming to discriminate between different cultural traditions in terms of their intrinsic worth are ruled out of order. Cultural diversity is an unqualified good; judgments of good or bad with respect to different cultures are condemned as cultural imperialism.

From the standpoint of the present essay, the important point to be made now is as follows: During the worldwide explosion of European political, commercial, and military power following the Enlightenment, Christian missions shared in this expansion. Christian missions were, in fact, among the main carriers of the ideas of the Enlightenment into the other continents. Through their schools, universities, hospitals, and training programs, they made widely available the new way of understanding the human situation. They were (in very many cases) quite happy to see their work as part of the civilizing mission of Europe. The churches of Europe and their cultural offshoots in the Americas had largely come to a kind of comfortable cohabitation with the Enlightenment, and there did not seem to be any contradiction in the combination of modern education, medicine, and technology with the proclamation of the gospel. It was almost inevitable that the collapse of confidence in the great project of the Enlightenment should carry with it a collapse of confidence in the validity of the church's worldwide missionary enterprise. Missionaries, often regarded as models of Christian devotion in the piety of the nineteenth century, are targets for ridicule or abuse in the public perception of the twentieth. They are (or were) the ignorant destroyers of precious native cultures and the bigoted agents of Christian churches, churches blind to the splendid diversity of human cultures and blinkered by their own dogma. It was therefore natural that multiculturalism should have, as one of its products, a multifaith ideology that rejoices in the multiplicity of religious beliefs and sees it as

33

an opportunity for mutual edification, to the disparagement of the use of the critical faculty.

This collapse has been extraordinarily swift. Perhaps I may be allowed to speak here of my own personal experience. When my wife and I went to India as missionaries in 1936, we were part of the ruling race. In the month-long voyage from Liverpool to Madras, I expected to see and saw the evidence of British presence at every port of call. In India I was a *sahib*. Of course, as a good liberal, I believed in and actively wrote and spoke for the independence of India. But that did not alter the fact that I was part of the ruling and "civilizing" race. In the closing years of our missionary service in Madras, during the 1970s, we were accustomed to the sight of young people from Britain and other European countries wandering in the streets as beggars clothed in unwashed Indian clothes. They were sadly seeking for the light that would give meaning to their lives, which had become empty of meaning, of purpose, and of hope.

Such loss of any sense of meaning in a culture that so recently believed itself to be the bearer of civilization for the world has been dramatic in its suddenness. Its most visible symptom is the enormous demand for drugs among the young people of the "developed" world, a demand which now fuels a huge international criminal enterprise. Many writers within the academic scene have described this loss of any sense of meaning. For example, Alan Bloom's *The Closing of the American Mind* is often quoted. He describes the total relativism into which his students have fallen. One does not speak of truth but of "what is true for me," or perhaps, "what is meaningful for me." The sense that there is a world beyond the self and that it is possible and also necessary to know this world beyond self becomes dim. Attention is concentrated on the self. Who am I? becomes an absorbing question, one that would never occur to a person who takes for granted the existence of a real world by which one can orient oneself. A small token of this is the reluctance to be known by anything beyond the given name — "Mary" or "John," for example. To give the family name, as has been customary in the past, would identify the individual by reference to a history and a society. But this is not acceptable. The self is an isolated monad which can only be understood from within itself. Thus the inward journey becomes much more fascinating than the exploration of an external world, and psychiatry becomes a dominant element in society.

This development must surely be recognized as a sign of impending death. Even the lowliest of animals survive only insofar as they are able to explore their environment and to discover where danger lies and where safety can be found. There is a real world to be explored and coped with, and one can be right or wrong about it. Survival depends on being right. Because, fortunately, human beings are not disembodied minds and we still have to live in the real world which we share with the rest of the animals, we cannot retreat into total subjectivity. If we are to survive, we are compelled to recognize that there is a difference between truth and falsehood in the statements we make about the world which is our environment. But our habits of thought do, in the long term, affect our ways of behaving, and this collapse into relativism and subjectivism must in the end disable us for survival. It is not surprising that we are now witnessing, in the form of religious fundamentalism, a world-wide reaction against this subjectivism. Precisely in those places where the most vigorous efforts have been made to implant the ideas and the practices of an enlightened secular society, there are strong movements of religious fundamentalism. Ever since the work of Max Weber on the subject, it has been widely believed that the progressive adoption by society of modern science, technology, and bureaucracy must necessarily lead to the progressive marginalization of religion and to its eventual extinction as a factor in international affairs. Secularization was regarded as an irreversible process and frequently, as in the

1960s, applauded as a movement of liberation. This is now seen to have been mistaken. Religious fundamentalism is now a powerful factor in public life, not least in the business of international politics. One may deplore this, but one cannot ignore it. It would seem that the human spirit cannot survive indefinitely without some kind of religion.

Looking back over the story told so far, it would seem that we have an example of the irony of human history. Modernity was born in a passion to seek and find absolute certainty. It saw science, in contrast to the generality of human knowledge, as an area of certainty. But this quest for indubitable certainty has led us to what seems to be an abandonment of the claim to be able to know the truth. If we are to find a way out of this blind alley, we must first look further at some of the consequences of the method of Descartes, which set in motion developments we have been surveying.

Once again we have to recognize that everything depends upon the chosen starting point. The starting point for Descartes was his own existence as a thinking mind. This was self-evident and indubitable truth. One can point out that it would have been equally possible to start with the self as acting or feeling or loving, and the existence of this self would have been equally indubitable. Descartes's choice of the thinking self as the starting point had the effect of opening up the three dualisms to which I have already referred and which we must discuss more fully:

1. The first is the dualism between the thinking mind and the world of things extended in space, between what Descartes called *res cogitans* and *res extensa*. Descartes did not believe that there could be such a thing as empty space; all space was something extended. The thinking mind was not extended in space. It was, so to speak, a single point, an eye looking from outside into the cosmos extended in space. The mental world and the world of material things belong, as it were, to two quite

36

platonic

different and separate realms of being. The material world is a closed entity. This has led to the popular idea that God, who belongs to the mental or spiritual world, cannot influence or interfere with the material world. The world of pure thought, as for example in mathematics, hovers above the "real" — that is, the material — world but is not part of it. This dualism is very similar to that which dominated classical thought, namely, the sharp distinction between a world of pure forms or ideas and the sensible world with which we are in contact through our five senses.

The early church had to overcome this dualism if it was to affirm as public truth the gospel's central statement that the *logos* was identical with the man Jesus of Nazareth. It could do so because the starting point of its thinking was in the Bible, where this dualism is absent. It formulated its rejection of the dualism in the statement that the one God was the creator of both the visible and invisible realities. So long as this dualism remains part of popular thought, as it still does, it is impossible for the gospel to be accepted as public truth; it can only be private opinion. The developments in physics and mathematics during the past one hundred years have been in the direction of overcoming this dualism. In quantum physics, the observer and the object of observation do not belong to separate worlds; they interact. But this and similar developments have not yet had time to penetrate and shape the way in which most people understand their world.

2. The second dualism, closely related to the first, is that dualism expressed by the words "objective" and "subjective." These words and the dichotomy that they describe have become so integral to our ways of speaking that it is very hard to think in a way that is not controlled by them. A little reflection, of course, will show that all human knowing involves both a knowing human subject and something that is the object of the subject's inquiry. These two poles, subject and object, constitute any knowing that takes place. But the method of Descartes has created a wide gulf between them, so that we have become accustomed to the idea that truth claims can be divided into those which communicate objective knowledge and those which express subjective experiences. Those who labored in the nineteenth century to propagate the opinion that science was the only avenue to objective truth and that it must therefore replace religion as the locus of public truth succeeded in implanting the objective-subjective dualism idea deep in the public mind. Claims to recognize beauty or goodness were treated as purely subjective: they expressed a feeling, an experience of the subject, but they did not give true information about a reality beyond the subject. On the other hand, the findings of science were offered (not by the leading scientists but by the popularizers of science) as objective facts that were universally true whatever the culture, the psychology, or the other contingent elements in the makeup of the human person. Once again, of course, this meant that the only possible locus of public truth was in the sciences. Religion could only be a matter of personal experience.

3. The third dualism was the dualism between *theoria* (theory) and *praxis* (practice). These two Greek words are absent from the Bible because they express a way of understanding things which is foreign to the Bible but which is now so deeply implanted in our culture that it is difficult to avoid using the two words. The words obviously belong to the dualistic worldview in which one first develops a mental picture of how things are and how they ought to be and then, as a second step, applies this picture to the "real" situation. There is a marked contrast between this way of thinking and that which we find in the Bible, where the way in which God makes himself known is not through vision but through hearing. Because the ultimate reality in the Bible is personal, we are brought into conformity with this reality not by the two-step process of theory and practice, vision and action, but by a single action comprised of hearing, believing, and obeying. The operative contrast is not between theory and practice; it is between believing and obeying on the one hand and the refusal of belief and obedience on the other. Believing and obeying are not two separate moves. When Jesus says to Simon, "Follow me," the response is a single act of faith and obedience; there is no gap between a mental action of believing and a bodily action of following. The human person is not a mind attached to a body but a single psychosomatic being. The implication of this, of course, is that the gospel does not become public truth for a society by being propagated as a theory or as a worldview and certainly not as a religion. It can become public truth only insofar as it is embodied in a society (the church) which is both "abiding in" Christ and engaged in the life of the world.

The present essay is concerned with the possibility of certain knowledge and especially with the possibility of confident knowledge of God. All three of the dualisms which I have described are relevant to this discussion, but perhaps the most important is the second of the three, the dualism of objective and subjective. The debate about Christian certainty is often polarized between those who wish to affirm the objective truth of the Christian claim to knowledge of God and those who deny it. But if this dualism is a false one, the whole debate is misguided. I have briefly referred to developments in science which have tended to bypass these dualisms, and it will now be helpful to refer to the work of one scientist who has focused attention particularly on this dualism. I refer to the Hungarian scientist Michael Polanyi, who used the term "personal knowledge" with the precise intention of affirming that the objective-subjective dualism is false and that all knowing of reality involves the personal commitment of the knower as a whole person.

Polanyi was a working scientist who had made several

important discoveries in the study of crystals. His was not the approach of the philosopher who asks, How can these truth claims be justified? but that of the research scientist who asks, How do we come to know, and how are discoveries made? Obviously, there are no rules for making new discoveries. Discovery means learning something new which was not known before. It involves a venture beyond what is known. How does it come about that discoveries in science are made? Polanyi's answer to this question involved, among other things, the following:

1. It involves apprenticeship to a tradition of knowledge. Learning is a skill which, like any other skill, cannot be acquired by the unaided mental processes of the student. It is acquired by working with and under the direction of those who are already skilled. No significant advances are made in science without a long and often arduous apprenticeship in the tradition of scientific work.

2. Scientists work by "indwelling" this tradition. The assumptions, the assured findings of the past, and the methods of science become part of their own equipment on which they rely. All this functions like the lenses of our spectacles. While we are wearing our usual spectacles and exploring the world around us, we do not attend to the lenses; we attend *through* them to the things we are examining. They function as an extension of the lenses in our own eyes, and we indwell them just as we indwell our own eyes. Likewise when we have come to use a language freely, we indwell the language. We do not look at the language as an object over against us; we think *through* the language. By indwelling it we are able to make contact with the world around us. We are subsidiarily aware of the words we use, but we focus on the things to which they refer. In the same way, scientists are subsidiarily aware of the tradition to which they are apprenticed while, at the same time, they are focally attending to the object of their research. If their work is to make progress, they have to trust this tradition, just as we have to trust the lenses in our eyes or in our spectacles. This trust is a precondition for our exploration of the world. The whole scientific tradition functions, according to Polanyi, as a "fiduciary framework"; it is something which we have to trust in order to make advances in knowledge.

3. Advances in scientific knowledge are made by recognizing a problem and seeking a solution. It may be a problem which no one has recognized before. But what exactly is a problem? Is it something known or something unknown? If it is known, why is there a problem? If it is unknown, how would we recognize a solution when we found it? The answer that Polanyi proposes to this old conundrum is as follows: Recognition of a problem is an awareness, an intuition, that there is something — a pattern or a harmony waiting to be found — hidden in the apparent haphazardness of empirical reality. This cannot be more than an intuition. And it may prove to have been an illusion. There have been scientists who have spent years seeking solutions to problems which were illusory. One might refer to the centuries of effort devoted to the discovery of perpetual motion or of the "philosopher's stone," but there are plenty of modern examples. Scientific discovery involves such gifts as intuition, imagination to project possible patterns, prudence coupled with a willingness to take risks, and courage and patience in pursuing a long and arduous course of investigation. At every point along this course, there is need of personal judgment in deciding whether a pattern is significant or merely random. None of these things can be covered by formal rules. They all involve the personal commitment of the scientist, and it is absurd to pretend that the findings of science can be understood without taking into account all these subjective factors.

4. From what has been said already it is clear that, in the work of the scientist, the focal point of attention has around it a vast area of what Polanyi calls "tacit knowledge." There is a

41

vast amount which we know, which in fact guides our thinking, but which we do not explicitly formulate. We know far more than we can express, and our formal and explicit knowledge depends upon a vast amount which is not formal and explicit. A boy of ten can ride a bicycle without being able to state explicitly the rules governing the relation between the turn he makes to keep his balance, the speed of the cycle, and the angle of disequilibrium. I can recognize my wife's face in a crowd of a thousand people, but I could not explicitly state the exact geometrical patterns of her features which enable me to do so. The explicit formulations of scientists rest upon this vast area of tacit knowledge which they share in greater or lesser degrees with all human beings.

5. That science will eventually enable us to understand everything in the visible world through the discovery of mass and energy laws governing the behavior of the smallest particles of matter, and that science will therefore enable us to eventually predict and control all events is an illusion. This idea, popularized in the nineteenth century, fails to recognize the hierarchical structure of the physical world. The movement of atomic particles sets limits to the possibilities of chemical combination, but the laws of chemistry cannot be limited to those of physics. The physical and chemical properties of the bones and muscles of an animal set limits on what it can do, but biology cannot be reduced to physics. So also, to come to a well-known example, the laws of mechanics set limits on what any machine can do, but they do not explain the purpose for which the machine was constructed. The exhaustive examination of the physical, chemical, and mechanical structure of the machine will not enable us to discover the purpose for which the machine was constructed. We have to be informed either by the designer of the machine or by someone who is accustomed to using it for its proper purpose. There is thus a hierarchy of levels of explanation, and this would naturally lead us further than Polanyi himself explic-

itly goes. But even at this stage it is worth noting that for an explanation of the purpose of the machine we depend upon a personal communication accepted in faith.

6. What, then, of the objectivity of our knowledge? It is obvious, for example, that when conservative Christians insist that their Christian faith refers to objective realities, they are (rightly) seeking to deny the opinion that these Christian beliefs are simply expressions of subjective feelings or experiences and to affirm that they make contact with a reality beyond the self. But it is also clear that it is futile to deny the subjective elements in the Christian's confession. How does Polanyi escape from the charge that his epistemology of science would reduce science to a matter of subjective experiences? Polanyi's answer is twofold: First, he says that, although all claims to know involve a personal commitment, the scientist makes them "with universal intent." He claims that they are true not just for himself but for everyone. For this reason he publishes them and invites all his colleagues to test and judge for themselves. Second, Polanyi says that the truth of the claim either will or will not be validated depending on whether or not it leads to further truth. A valid truth claim will lead to new discovery — often to discoveries undreamt of by the scientist themselves. The truth claims of scientists are thus not irreformable and indubitable claims to possess the truth; rather, they are claims to be on the way to the fullness of truth. There is thus no absolute dichotomy, such as Descartes has bequeathed to us, between knowing and believing. Knowing always involves the personal commitments of the knowers, for which they are prepared to risk their careers as scientists.

In one of the most concise statements of his position, Polanyi, after speaking of "the personal participation of the knower in all acts of understanding," goes on:

> But this does not make our understanding *subjective*. Comprehension is neither an arbitrary act nor a passive experience,

but a responsible act claiming universal validity. Such knowledge is indeed *objective* in the sense of establishing contact with a hidden reality, contact that is defined as the condition for anticipating an indeterminate range of as yet unknown (and perhaps yet inconceivable) true implications. It seems reasonable to describe this fusion of the personal and the objective as personal knowledge. (Polanyi, *Personal Knowledge,* pp. vii-viii)

Polanyi's concern was to alert the scientific community to a danger which, if not faced, would destroy it. But his thinking has obvious relevance to the subject of this essay. In the debate which goes on among religious people about the respective roles of faith and doubt in the search for certainty, Polanyi invites us to consider whether we are not operating with an entirely false and deceptive idea of certainty. It is the dominance in the public mind of this false and illusory ideal of certainty which hopelessly confuses the debate among Christians about the certainty of their faith.

4

Knowing God

A disastrous shift in the way science was being understood and practiced, experienced by Polanyi especially through his contacts with the Soviet leadership during the 1930s, prompted him to move from the work of research science to the study and teaching of philosophy. The Soviet leaders regarded science simply as a necessary tool for the implementation of their social planning. The idea that pure science should be practiced as an avenue to truth was dismissed as bourgeois nonsense. Science was a necessary instrument in the pursuit of power. And it was obvious that the Russians were only pushing more logically in the direction that was being taken elsewhere. Polanyi had to ask himself, "What are the grounds for believing that the findings of science are not merely useful but true?" In the attempt to answer this question, he came to the conclusion that we had been misled by the illusion of a totally objective knowledge. If objectivity means that we must aim for the greatest possible truthfulness in our thinking and speaking about realities beyond our own minds, then of course it is a proper goal. But if it means that all subjective elements are excluded, then it is obviously absurd to suppose that total objectivity is possible; for, if there is no subject who knows, there is no knowing. As we have seen, Polanyi used the term "personal knowledge" to designate a conception of knowledge as the responsible activity of a person who is required to make costly and risky commitments. In the growing atmosphere of nihilism, Polanyi sought to reaffirm the possibility and the necessity that we should have the courage to confidently affirm beliefs which can be doubted; and he strived to show that the idea of a certainty which relieves us of the need for personal commitment is an illusion.

This illusion is so much part of the accepted worldview of modern societies that it is not easy to separate oneself from it. Its debilitating effect on the articulation of the Christian faith in contemporary Western society is so far-reaching that it affects all levels of the life of the church. At the popular level, it is assumed that Christianity is merely one of a class of opinions called religious and must be described as such in public discussion. Thus Christianity is looked at from outside, from the point of view of a generally accepted belief about a world of facts which are neutral in their relation to the varieties of religion. At the academic level, a distinction is made between the confessional and the scientific study of theology. The scarcely concealed assumption is that the word "scientific" refers to a kind of study which has no prior commitments about the nature of truth but has a totally open mind, as though the scientific mind were a sort of empty page on which nothing had already been written. The truth, of course, is that both approaches — the confessional and the scientific — presuppose (as all rational inquiry must presuppose) a long tradition of thought and practice that determines which beliefs are plausible and which are not.

But we are now entering a postmodern period, a time in which the seemingly assured assumptions we have inherited from the Enlightenment are being deconstructed. The assumptions of the modern scientific worldview can no longer be taken as secure foundations. Everyone recognizes that science works; it delivers desirable things. But we are left in a world which the Chinese writer Carver Yu has summarized in the phrase "technological optimism and literary despair." Looking at contemporary Western society from his standpoint as a Chinese philosopher and theologian, he sees not only the unstoppable dynamism of our science-based technology but also the bleak nihilism and hopelessness that is reflected in the literature, art, and drama of our society. Science combines to deliver an ever-growing abundance of things to have and to do, beyond all the dreams of earlier ages. It offers no guidance, however, on the questions of worth: What things are worth doing? What things are worth having? Perhaps the most poignant example of this tragic situation is the way in which the wizardry of satellite television is now employed to pour a cataract of trash into every living room. In the 28th chapter of Job, the glowing description of the marvels of human technology is followed by the haunting question: "But where shall wisdom be found?" This same question haunts us today. How can it become possible to affirm confidently as public truth the reality of those things which are not amenable to the tests Descartes laid down for certain truth? How can we speak confidently about truth, beauty, and goodness when we know that what we say can always be doubted?

Polanyi was seeking to articulate a position which would make possible confident affirmation of belief in matters which can be doubted. His explorations ranged beyond the work of the natural sciences and into the areas of public debate about the life of society as a whole. He did not directly extend his work into the area of theology, but it obviously has very direct relevance to my present discussion of the possibility of confidence in theological discourse. More specifically, Polanyi's concept of personal knowledge has four particularly important implications for theology.

Polanyi points out that knowing is always part of a tradition. The mental activity involved in trying to make reliable contact with reality can function only by indwelling a tradition of language, concepts, models, images, and assumptions of many kinds which function as the lenses through which we try to find

47

out what is really there. The critical movement initiated by Descartes sought to subject all tradition to questioning and to build a structure of knowledge which would be accredited by pure unaided reason, having the precision and the certainty of mathematics. Polanyi says that the period following Descartes has been the most brilliant in all human history, but he also adds: "Its incandescence has fed on the combustion of the Christian heritage in the oxygen of Greek rationalism, and when the fuel was exhausted the critical framework burned away" (*Personal Knowledge*, p. 265). This is why Polanyi describes his work as an attempt to develop a "postcritical philosophy." No one can deny the achievements of the critical period. But it was a mistake to suppose that the enterprise of knowing the reality of which we are a part can begin, so to speak, with an empty page, that it can take off from an act of pure thought. With hindsight, it is now easy to see how many of the self-evident truths of the Enlightenment were self-evident only to those who were the heirs of a thousand years of Christian teaching. They were not self-evident to the peoples of India or Africa. The critical movement intended to clear the ground of beliefs and superstitions inherited from the past so that it could create a structure of indubitable truth; instead, the movement has ended by creating a vacant site into which new follies and superstitions are crowding. Could the leaders of the Age of Reason have ever imagined that, two centuries after their work, the forces of astrology, witchcraft, and black magic would once again capture hearts and minds in a Europe that enjoyed, at the same time, just that universal public education which was one of their dreams?

At this point, Polanyi refers to Augustine's dictum "I believe in order to know" and points out that, while both faith and critical reason have necessary roles to play in the enterprise of knowing, modern man has renounced the first of these and left himself bereft of the possibility of knowing anything. But we cannot simply go back.

We have plucked from the tree a second apple which has forever imperilled our knowledge of good and evil, and we must learn to know these qualities henceforward in the blinding light of our new analytical powers. . . . Innocently we had trusted that we could be relieved of all personal responsibility for our beliefs by objective criteria of validity — and our own critical powers have shattered this hope.

In this situation, what Polanyi is doing is

seeking to restore to us once more the power for the deliberate holding of unproven beliefs. We should be able to profess now knowingly and openly those beliefs which could be tacitly taken for granted in the days before modern philosophic criticism reached its present incisiveness. Such powers may appear dangerous. But a dogmatic orthodoxy can be kept in check both internally and externally, while a creed inverted into a science is both blind and deceptive. (*Personal Knowledge,* p. 268)

This blind and deceptive creed, presenting itself as knowledge in contrast to belief, inhibits Christians from confidently affirming their faith as something which provides the criteria for judging all other claims to knowledge and which does not itself submit to judgment by this other creed, the inverted into science.

All efforts to know must begin with something given. This given includes what we normally call the data, the facts that form part of the foundation from which our reason works. It also includes, as previously argued, the tradition of knowing which has been developed in a human community and which includes the language and all the conceptual tools used in that tradition. All of these constitute the given elements that are the precondition for any rational thought. And all of this can be the object of critical questioning. It is not self-evident truth. Specifically, Christian thinking stands in the tradition of discipleship (a matter of both thought and action) stemming from the acts of God, these acts being the substance of the good news communicated by the church. In a society that has accepted another creed, the "blind and deceptive" creed referred to by Polanyi, and that — moreover — does not recognize it as a creed but thinks that it is a religiously neutral account of the facts, confident affirmation of the Christian faith as public truth is regarded as sectarian and dogmatic. And this charge comes precisely from those who have accepted the reigning dogma of their society without question.

The dependence of all systematic thought upon assumptions that are accepted by faith has been well documented in the work of the American philosopher Roy Clouser. In his book *The Myth of Religious Neutrality* (1991), he examines major theories in the areas of mathematics, physics, and psychology and shows how all such theories involve a prior decision as to what is fundamental in the area studied. If we define the word *Theos* as that on which everything else depends but which itself depends on nothing else — a reasonable definition — then none of these scientific theories is theologically neutral. All of them rest on fundamental assumptions which can be questioned. But the questioning, if it is to be rational, has to rely on other fundamental assumptions which can in turn be questioned. It follows (and this is Polanyi's point) that there can be no knowing without personal commitment. We must believe in order to know.

Polanyi emphasizes the fact that knowing is a form of activity. Like all activity, it involves the interaction of the person with a word beyond him or her. It is an activity which (as we have seen) involves the whole person in a passionate commitment to make contact with reality. Knowing is not something that happens to us; it is something we seek to achieve. As with all activities, there is always the possibility of failure. "The possibility of error is a necessary element of any belief bearing on reality, and to withhold belief on the grounds of such a hazard is to break off all contact with reality" (Polanyi, *Personal Knowledge,* p. 315).

The certainty that Descartes sought and claimed to have achieved is thus available only within a mental world that is not in contact with a reality beyond itself. His "I think, therefore I am" may be indubitable, but it makes no contact with anything beyond his own mind. We meet again the radical dualism between the mental world and the material world which is so fundamental in the legacy of Descartes. It is natural in this dualistic world that mathematics is seen as the necessary language of certain scientific knowledge, for mathematics operates in a mental world detached from anything outside the mind. Even as a schoolboy learning Euclid, I remember reflecting (perhaps because my pencil was blunt) that there is really no such thing as a point which has position but no dimensions or a line which had length but no breadth. All the elements in Euclidean geometry are ideal concepts which can only be related to material realities by approximation. The certainty of mathematical propositions, as Einstein often observed, is strictly proportionate to their remoteness from reality. That the only objective and therefore reliable knowledge is that furnished by science and that the proper form of scientific statements is mathematical — these are the popular ideas, so dominant in modern societies, that continue to inhibit us from making confident statements of (for example) religious faith because they are not amenable to this form of statement. Kurt Gödel's demonstration that the fundamental axioms of mathematics are not self-justifying does not seem to have weakened the influence of the idea of mathematical certainty.

But we are moving into a postmodern era. This morning, as I am writing these words, there is much anxious discussion in the news both among leaders of the British Association for the Advancement of Science and in the government about how to arrest the growing disinclination of students to take up science for their university studies. The only solutions offered consist of ways to make scientific work more financially lucrative. It does not seem to occur to those I heard on a news program this morning that there may be a deep and growing skepticism about science as a whole, and about its capacity to give meaning to human life even if it should prove to be financially rewarding. Polanyi draws attention to the lessons to be learned from the collapse of Greek mathematics after the death of Apollonius in 205 B.C. and speculates about the possibility of a similar collapse in our day (*Personal Knowledge,* pp. 192-93). What is clear is that the Cartesian confidence in mathematics as the locus of certainty is part of the same dualism that dominated classical thought, the dualism that separated a world of pure forms known by the mind from the world of material things known through our senses. Certainty belongs to the former, not to the latter. Only statements that can be doubted make contact with reality.

In his parable of the oxygen and the fuel, Polanyi speaks of the combustion of the Christian heritage in the oxygen of Greek rationalism. That heritage is essentially a story, the story told in the Bible. The community of the Christian church understands itself and the human and cosmic history of which it is part in terms of the biblical story. Its being and life are incomprehensible apart from this story. Its liturgical actions are the reliving of this story. Of course we have to recognize that Christianity as it has developed and changed over the centuries has much in common with other religions, with various philosophies, and with various worldviews. But Christianity, as it presents itself at any time or place in history for inspection as an empirical reality, is always subject to judgment and correction in the light of that which it seeks to express and to embody, namely, God's actions for the creation and redemption of the world. The gospel, the account of these actions, is always in narrative form: "The Word became flesh," "God so loved the world that he gave his one and only Son. . . ," and so forth. The ecumenical creeds are also in narrative form. Above all, the Bible, taken as a whole and in its canonical form, is a unique interpretation of cosmic and human history in which the human person is seen as a responsible actor in human history, always being called to respond to the initiatives of the one who is both Creator and Savior. This book is unique. None of the other sacred scriptures of the world's great religions have a character anything like this. And it was this narrative which made Europe a cultural entity distinct from Asia, of which it was and is simply a peninsula.

It would contradict the whole message of the Bible itself if one were to speak of the book apart from the church, the community shaped by the story that the book tells. For more than one thousand years, during which the successive waves of invaders from Asia were slowly schooled into a new society, the Bible was the place where reliable truth was to be found. In the absence of printing, of course, it was not in the hands of more than a few scholars. But through the liturgy and preaching of the church and through all the avenues of art, drama, and popular festival, it provided the framework through which the world and its affairs were understood. And, of course, this understanding was not merely an intellectual affair. It was part of a total way of life, corporate and individual. The church was the bearer of the story. The story shaped the church. As a continually lived narrative, of which contemporary life was a part, the narrative gave shape to public life.

It is impossible to understand the distinctive character of Europe, that which makes it different (in spite of great internal diversity) from Asia or Africa, without grasping the uniqueness of this narrative. What makes the narrative unique is the character of the One who is the chief actor in the whole story, God — the God of Abraham, of Israel, of Jesus. Of course there is nothing unique about the word "God." There is, I suppose, no human language on earth which does not have a word which can be plausibly translated as "God." At least the Bible Societies have not yet found one. But, in terms of sovereignty over all creation and all history, there is nothing comparable to the God of the Bible. Throughout vast tracts of Asian culture the ultimate reality is not a personal God at all but such impersonal entities as *Dharma*, the *Tao*, or that ultimate reality of whom the Upanishads can only say *Neti, neti*- "not that, not that." Even when, as in many forms of Indian religion, there is a strong sense of a personal God to whom loving devotion is due, there is not the sharply etched and unforgettably real character that we recognize in the God of the Bible. No one who has been deeply immersed in the biblical narrative could ever again entirely escape from the presence of that One, God, so tender and yet so terrible, so passionate in his wrathful love and his loving wrath, forever calling on those who turn their backs on him, forever humbling himself in tender appeal, forever challenging his children to the heights of utter purity, and finally accepting the shameful death of a condemned sinner in order to open for us the gate of glory. There is absolutely nothing in all the world's sacred scriptures that can be compared for a moment with this. And a society that has lived with this God for more than a thousand years can never, even when revolting against him, wholly cast off that memory. It can never again be sunk into the half-light of impersonal pantheism or primitive polytheism.

Now the point to be made here is as follows: A story cannot provide the kind of indubitable certainty which was the ideal of Descartes. As Lessing said, accidental happenings of history cannot prove eternal truths of reason. If we are in search of the kind of indubitable certainty which Descartes claimed, the Bible must be set aside. The Bible claims to be a true interpretation of universal history. Since we are not yet at the end of history and since it may yet contain many surprises, we cannot have indubitable certainty. The only possible responses to the claims that the Bible makes are belief or unbelief. There can be no indubitable proofs. No one has seen God so as to verify the claim that he exists. No one has seen the end of the world so as to be sure of the direction in which we have to go. There is no scientific way of testing the claims and promises that the Bible makes. There is no way of being indubitably certain that this is what history is really about and that this gives us the direction of our lives. It must be, as the church has always said, a matter of divine revelation accepted in faith (John 1:18).

But this, of course, is what the Age of Reason rejected. It saw reason and revelation as mutually opposed and called upon human beings to be bold enough to use their reason, to put away a childish dependence on divine revelation, and to use the God-given gift of reason to establish the facts for themselves. The question to be asked is, What do we mean by "the facts"? In an amusing phrase, Alasdair MacIntyre says that "fact" in modern parlance is "a folk concept with an aristocratic ancestry," the aristocrat in question being Lord Bacon, who advised his contemporaries to "abjure speculation and collect facts" (MacIntyre, *After Virtue,* p. 7). In using the term "speculation" Bacon referred to the universals of classical and medieval philosophy, such as essence, existence, substance, cause, and purpose. By "facts" he meant things which, unlike these others, are tangible and measurable. The original meaning of the word is, as I said earlier, that of the Latin *factum,* "something which has been done, or accomplished." In this original sense, one may properly say that the gospel is a statement of facts, of what God has done. But in the contemporary folk usage, of course, the gospel is not about facts.

With respect to the speculations he rejected, however, it is important to note that Bacon did retain one of these universals. He rejected the concept of purpose as a category of explanation but retained the concept of cause. This has had momentous consequences for the subsequent history of science. Even though in later philosophy the concept of cause has been rejected (David Hume), it has played a central role in the development of science. To understand the causes of things or to unravel the cause-effect linkages between different things is, in popularized science, to explain them. It is to show how things work. But to understand the purpose for which things exist has not been part of the work of science. Even in the study of animal behavior, where it would seem natural to the unscientific mind to say that birds build their nests for the purposes of hatching and protecting their young, it is thought by (at least) some scientists that this is an unscientific way of talking and that the behavior of birds can be explained without the use of this concept. And in the much wider field of evolutionary studies, some scientists seek to explain the whole story of the genesis and development of human life as being entirely due to the operation of impersonal causes — though they often forget their principles by letting slip such phrases as "Nature has made provision for . . . ," or "natural selection has seen to it that. . . ." If nature is the ultimate reality with which we have to deal, then — almost inevitably — nature has to be personified.

The elimination of the concept of purpose from our efforts to understand the world has momentous consequences. With one stroke it creates the split between fact and value, a split which is such an important part of our culture. The reason why it causes this split is obvious. If one has no idea of the purpose for which a thing exists, one cannot say whether it is good or bad. It may be good for some purposes but not for others. It has been a central axiom of modernity that one cannot argue from a statement of fact to a judgment of value.

MacIntyre counters this with an example: "This watch has not lost ten seconds in five years; therefore, it is a good watch." To most people this would seem an obvious contradiction of the fact-value dichotomy. But, as MacIntyre points out, we only move from the factual statement to the value judgment because we take it for granted that a watch is understood to be an instrument for measuring time. It is defined by its purpose. But if a visitor from outer space who had never seen a watch and had no idea whether it was for decorating the living room or for throwing at the cat were told that it had not lost ten seconds in five years, he would have no grounds for the conclusion, "It is a good watch." The visitor could discover by examination what made the watch work. He could discover, given time, all the causeeffect links from the tension on the spring to the movements of the hands on the face of the watch. Observation and reason would be enough for him to, in these terms, explain the watch without leaving any unsolved puzzles. But this research would not enable him to discover the purpose for which these pieces of metal were put together in this particular way. For him to discover this, someone would have to tell him — either the maker of the watch, or someone who was accustomed to using it for its proper purpose. In other words, he would have to depend on a personal communication or revelation. And he would have to accept this, at least initially, by faith in the one who told him.

Cause is something that can be discovered by observation and reason. Purpose is not available for inspection because, until the purpose has been realized, it is hidden in the mind of the one whose purpose it is. Suppose that going along a street, we observe men at work with piles of bricks and bags of cement, and we guess that a building is being erected. What is it to be? An office? A house? A chapel? There are only two ways to discover the answer: we can wait around until the work is complete and inspection enables us to discover what it is. If we cannot wait until then, we must ask the architect, and we will have to take his word for it. If the work in question is not the building of a house but the creation and consummation of the cosmos, the first alternative is not available to us. We shall not be present to examine the end product of cosmic history. *If* the whole thing has any purpose (and of course we may decide, as postmoderns do, that it has no purpose), the only way we can know that purpose is by a disclosure from the one whose purpose it is, a disclosure which we would have to take on trust. There is no escape from this necessity. The modern antithesis of observation and reason on the one hand versus revelation and faith on the other is only tenable on the basis of a prior decision that the whole cosmic and human story has no purpose and therefore no meaning. It is possible to make this assumption, but it is not necessary. The question whether the cosmos and human life within it have any purpose other than the individual purposes we seek to impose on things is one that cannot be decided by observation. If we live with a prior assumption that human life has no purpose; then we shall act accordingly, and there will be no possibility whatsoever of discovering its purpose. As I have argued, only by an act of disclosure of the purpose of human life can we learn that it indeed has a purpose, and such an act of disclosure can only be personal, a revelation. Here we have what William James called a "closed option." There is no possibility of keeping an open mind. We have to act in order to live, and our actions will be determined by whether we believe the universe embodies a purpose other than our own or do not so believe. There is no third possibility.

Polanyi used the phrase "personal knowledge" to define an understanding of human knowing that transcends the false dichotomy of objective and subjective. The argument I have pursued now brings me to the point where I have to ask whether or not we must recognize our knowing as personal knowledge in a further sense. Our argument leads to the suggestion that our knowing of reality will be defective if it does not recognize that this reality is only fully explicable by reference to a personal being. (I use the word "suggestion," not "proof.") This would lead to the thought that Polanyi's conception of a hierarchy of levels of explanation has to include a level beyond those we considered when discussing this part of Polanyi's thought. Atomic structure determines the way in which matter behaves and therefore defines the limits of what chemical configurations are possible, but it does not itself explain these configurations. Therefore, chemistry cannot be reduced to physics. Similarly, biology cannot be reduced to chemistry or to mechanics, although the behavior of all living animals is limited by the atomic, chemical, and mechanical features of their makeup. So also, to use the key example of Polanyi, the structure and composition of a machine can be explained in terms of the laws governing the physical and chemical properties of its parts, but these laws cannot explain the proper functioning of the machine; this can only be explained in terms of the purpose of the one who designed and constructed the machine. The physical, chemical, mechanical, and biological principles are all valid and necessary at their respective levels but are not adequate at the levels above them. Failure to recognize this is the fallacy in all forms of reductionism.

Therefore, if we are prepared to entertain and act on the possibility that the entire cosmos exists for some purpose and is not a chaos of purely random events, it follows that we have to recognize an upper level of explanation, namely, the theological level. We cannot have a total understanding of things without the cultivation of that particular kind of understanding which is concerned with knowing the nature and purpose of the One whose purpose is being realized in the entire history of the cosmos. Without calling into question the proper competence of all the lower levels of explanation — physical, chemical, biological, mechanical, sociological, and so forth — we must also acknowledge the proper role of theological inquiry as an essential part in the whole enterprise of human knowing.

At this point it is necessary to interject a caution. As for me and (I suspect) many in my generation, one of the crucial insights that made it possible to come to Christian faith was that of Martin Buber in his book *I and Thou*. Buber brilliantly expounded the radical difference between two kinds of knowing: that in which I am the masterful actor handling inert material which I am free to interrogate, to manipulate, and to organize, and that in which I am seeking to know another person who can resist my efforts to know and who can interrogate me and make me the object of inquiry. At a time when a reductionist interpretation of science prevented me, like others, from believing in the possibility of God, this opened up a new view of the possibility of knowledge. But this distinction between two kinds of knowing, immensely important as it was, could also lead to a false separation. All our interpersonal relations are made possible by the mediation of material realities through sight, sound, and touch. They are made possible by the fact that, as persons, we share a common world of impersonal realities. To abstract ourselves from this shared world is impossible. The attempt to isolate a personal relationship from its actual context in realities of an impersonal kind leads into serious error. A bizarre example of this was the movement known as group dynamics in which people were asked to interact with each other in the absence of any given impersonal reality, such as a subject for discussion. For those who were not robust enough to dismiss the enterprise as absurd, it led to real damage.

The importance of this for the present discussion, however, is as follows: if we speak of the theological level as the highest level of explanation, we must not mean that theological explanation is allowed to invade the proper territory of the lower levels; they have a proper, God-given autonomy, though it is not an absolute autonomy. To absolutize the autonomy of a lower level is reductionism. Because, as Christian faith affirms, the cosmos is a creation by a personal God and not an emanation from an impersonal absolute, it has a relative autonomy given to it by its creator. This, as I have noted earlier, is one of the four basic

creation principles expounded by the fourth century theologians, and without it the development of science would have been
impossible. We are given the responsibility of discovering the
principles which operate at each of the levels of explanation.
Theology cannot take over the business of physics or, for that
matter, of economics. We have to understand as much as
possible both the laws of physics and the laws of economics,
but it may also be necessary to have in mind the laws operating
at different levels. The breakdown of a machine may be due
simply to a defect in one of its parts: the material used was not
strong enough for the part's function in the machine. But the
breakdown may also be caused by using the machine for a
purpose for which it was not designed. In that case, replacement
of the worn-out part will not solve the problem. The breakdown
of an economic order, such as we are witnessing in this last
decade of the twentieth century, may perhaps be explained by
failures to understand the way the economy works: there are
indeed many (mutually contradictory) diagnoses being offered.
It may also be due to a failure to recognize the purpose for which
human life exists; the explanation could be theological. But even
good theology cannot replace good economics.

Polanyi's reflections on the nature of scientific knowledge
suggest a further step in our thinking about the nature of personal knowledge. Polanyi's argument opens the way for an exploration of a higher level of explanation which we would have
to describe as the theological level, that is to say, the level at
which we seek to know the purpose for which things exist. This,
as I have said, implies a further extension of the range of the
term "personal" with respect to our knowledge, including our
knowledge of impersonal realities. The implication is that all our
knowing is personal, not only in the sense that it involves the
personal and passionate commitment of the knower but also in
the sense that our knowledge will not be complete unless it
presses beyond the impersonal realities (explored with the tools

of physics, chemistry, biology, and the human sciences) to that personal reality which alone can carry a purpose for the whole, since purpose is a personal category. As I have said, Polanyi opens up the possibility and indeed the necessity of such a further move, but he does not himself enter into specifically theological discussion.

But there is one point in his work where this possibility and necessity seem remarkably clear. In *The Tacit Dimension* (1966), Polanyi addresses the question to which I have already referred: What is a problem? Scientific discovery begins with the recognition of a problem. If the work of the scientist is to be fruitful, the problem must be a good one; for there have been problems which have exercised human minds for long periods but which turn out to be no good, in the sense that the pursuit of a solution leads nowhere. But what *is* a problem? To recognize a problem, says Polanyi, is "to have an intimation of the coherence of hitherto not comprehended particulars," and the problem is good if this intimation is true. To recognize a good problem is thus to see something which is hidden, and not visible.

This, however, is a self-contradiction. How is it to be explained? This and the question, What is a problem? were addressed long ago by Plato in the Meno. His answer was that all discovery was a remembering of past lives. Modern science, born and bred in a society that rejected this ancient Asian concept, has never accepted Plato's explanation but has gone on cheerfully making discoveries in spite of the logical absurdity involved. Polanyi's explanation is to acknowledge the power of the human mind to recognize "intimations of things hidden which we may yet discover" (*The Tacit Dimension*, pp. 21-23). The immediate implication which Polanyi draws is that, if all our knowledge is to be of the kind sought by Descartes, namely, certain knowledge capable of explicit formulation in precise terms, then scientific discovery will be forever impossible. But

62

is it not legitimate to suggest a further implication? Polanyi depicts scientists engaged in research as being continually drawn forward by the intimation of patterns of coherence and intellectual beauty hitherto never explicitly stated. In this sense, scientists must be seen as people drawn by a reality beyond themselves. Is it not reasonable, then, to think of this reality as something more than a lifeless, impersonal "something"? Scientists, and indeed all serious scholars, speak often of the love of truth. But can love be finally satisfied with an impersonal "something"? Have we, perhaps, failed to draw out the full meaning of the words spoken by the apostle Paul to the scholars and debaters of Athens when he said that "the God who made the world and everything in it . . . . did this so that men would seek him and perhaps reach out for him and find him, though he is not far from each one of us" (Acts 17:24, 27)?

Here I can only answer that question by speaking of the fundamental affirmation of the gospel, namely, that the ultimate reality which is the object of all our search for truth has been made present in history in the person and work of Jesus Christ. "The Word was made flesh and dwelt among us . . . and we beheld his glory" (John 1:14). If that is true, then it must define the nature of all our search for truth, including our searches for truth in the world of impersonal entities. The theological level of inquiry, while not invading or calling into question the other levels on which explanation is to be sought, must be recognized as the ultimate one.

And this has immediate relevance to our contemporary situation. I have referred to the disquieting signs of a loss of faith in science. The debate sparked by Bryan Appleyard's book *Understanding the Present* (1992) must be continued. No one doubts that science has brought immense benefits to humanity. No one wishes to be excluded from these benefits. And yet there is profound uneasiness concerning what science and the technology it has made possible are doing to us all. Polanyi's voice was an early cry intended to alert us to the danger that would destroy science if it was not faced. The debate between science and the Christian faith has for too long been overdramatized and radically skewed by those who want to propose science as the replacement for an outworn faith. The time has come when both scientists and theologians must address the question, Can science be redeemed?

But this brings us to the point at which we must recognize that the scope of the discussion has been too limited. There is a dimension of the question that we have not yet touched, and we must now enter into a discussion of it.

5

By Grace Alone

I have tried to show that it is unreasonable to set up an opposition between observation and reason on the one hand, and revelation and faith on the other. I have argued that to shut out the possibility of revelation is to exclude at the outset the possibility that the cosmos might embody a purpose distinct from the various human purposes we bring to our encounter with it. But I have spoken as though revelation was, so to speak, a matter of giving information about what we would not be able to find out for ourselves. Revelation is indeed this, but it is this only because it is something much more. The revelation of which we speak in the Christian tradition is more than the communication of information; it is the giving of an invitation. It is more than an unfolding of the purpose, which was otherwise hidden in the mind of God but is now made known to us through God's revealing acts; it is also a summons, a call, an invitation. If we may refer to my rather crude parable of the building site — the Builder is not merely telling us what he is building; he is calling us to be builders with those whom he has already recruited. The response that is called for, therefore, is not only intellectual assent but also active response. It is belief and obedience, and the two are but two sides of one response. It is not that we are given a vision of the new world which God purposes and then consider how we might translate this vision into practical action.

We are not given a theory which we then translate into practice. Instead, we are invited to respond to a word of calling by believing and acting, specifically, by becoming part of the community which is already committed to the service of the Builder. We are invited to commit ourselves and to learn as we go what our role in the whole enterprise is to be. Our commitment is an act of personal faith. There is no possibility of the kind of indubitable certainty that Descartes claimed and that has been the criterion (spoken or assumed) for reliable knowledge in modern society. There is no insurance against risk. We are invited to make a personal commitment to a personal Lord and to entrust our lives to his service. We are promised that as we so commit ourselves we shall be led step-by-step into a fuller understanding of the truth.

All of this is canonically embodied in the words that are so central in the gospel narrative: "Follow me." At the beginning of his ministry, Jesus addresses these words to his first disciples, and their response is a single act which is both faith and obedience. At the end, when the mission of Jesus seems to have led into the darkness of total disaster, Jesus again assures Peter that, although Peter cannot follow his master now, he will follow afterwards; and when Thomas asks, "How can we know the way?" Jesus answers, "I am the way, and the truth, and the life" (John 14:6). Christian discipleship is not a two-stage affair in which a concept of truth is first formulated and is then translated into a program for action. It is a single action of faith and obedience to a living person, the response to a personal calling.

If we are to use the word "certainty" here, then it is not the certainty of Descartes. It is the kind of certainty expressed in such words as those of the Scriptures: "I know whom I have believed, and I am sure that he is able to guard until that day what has been entrusted to me" (2 Tim. 1:12). Note here two features of this kind of assurance which distinguish it from the ideal of certainty we have inherited from the Age of Reason.

In the first place, the locus of confidence (if one may put it so) is not in the competence of our own knowing, but in the faithfulness and reliability of the one who is known. The weight of confidence rests there and not here with us. Secondly, the phrase "until that day" reminds us that this is not a claim to possess final truth but to be on the way that leads to the fullness of truth. I do not *possess* the truth, so that I do not need to be open to new truth; rather, I am confident that the one in whom I have placed my trust, the one to whom I am committed, is able to bring me to the full grasp of what I now only partly understand.

This suggestion seem congruous with the teaching of the New Testament about the work of the Holy Spirit in leading the followers of Jesus into the fullness of truth. While the incarnation of the Word is an event in past history, not something which we search out and look for in the future, we are promised the help of the living Spirit who is the Spirit of God and the Spirit of Jesus, to enable us to draw out the meaning of that which has been given once and for all in the incarnation and to explore the ultimate limits of space and time with the aid of the divine Spirit. And this has immediate consequences.

This is the kind of certainty that is available to the Christian and in which he or she may rest. And surely it *must* be an illusion to imagine that there can be available to us a kind of certainty that does *not* involve this personal commitment. This at least must surely be said: if the biblical depiction of the human situation is true; *if* the supreme reality is a personal God whose we are and to whom we are responsible; then there is something quite absurd about the posture of those who claim infallible certainty about God in their own right and on the strength of their own rational powers. In our interpersonal relations, we would never make such a claim for our knowledge of another person. How absurd to make such a claim with respect to God!

But there is still something more, much more, to be said here. When we speak of God's self-revelation, we are certainly speaking of more than information and even invitation: we are speaking of reconciliation, of atonement, and of salvation. Our discussion so far has assumed that we are, so to speak, competent to undertake the search for truth — this has been the unquestioned assumption of modernity. The central conviction of the Enlightenment was that human reason, once liberated from the shackles of tradition, superstition, and religion, was capable of coming to the knowledge of the truth. The call, so often heard in ringing tones, to "follow truth at all costs," assumed that we are so made that we know what it is that we are seeking and that we shall recognize it when we find it. Here we have to come to that part of the whole Christian tradition against which the Age of Reason most strenuously took up arms. At the heart of the story of the ministry of Jesus as interpreted by the Fourth Evangelist, there occurs an encounter between Jesus and those of his hearers who had believed in him. It is reported that he said, "If you continue in my teaching, you are really my disciples. Then you will know the truth, and the truth will make you free" (John 8:31). Here we seem to have a direct reversal of one of the axioms of modernity, namely, that freedom of inquiry, freedom to think and speak and publish, is the way — the only way — to the truth. Jesus appears to reverse this. Truth is not a fruit of freedom; it is the precondition for freedom. It is not surprising that it was these words of Jesus which (according to the Fourth Gospel) precipitated an attempt to kill him. His hearers rightly perceived that he was telling them that they were not, as they believed, free. They were in bondage to sin, and only the truth could set them free. And he, Jesus, was the one whose word was truth and who could therefore set them free.

Here we have the most radical attack possible on the assumptions of modernity. To state the situation straightforwardly, this attack can hardly fail to rouse the same kind of anger in contemporary society as it did among those who heard those words of Jesus. Perhaps nowhere is this anger more deep today than among those Christians who have sought (with the truly admirable intention of making the gospel acceptable to the modern world) to commend Christianity as a tenable belief within the liberal assumptions of modern society. This helps to explain the strength, even ferocity, of liberal denunciations of what is called "fundamentalism." We cannot evade the sharpness of the issue here posed.

The anger of Jesus' hearers was to culminate in the events of Good Friday, when the living Truth was utterly rejected. Those who took up stones to kill Jesus rightly perceived that he was denying their claim to be free. "The Jews" in this text, as always in the Fourth Gospel, represent the world which does not acknowledge Jesus. That world is not free as it thinks it is. We are not honest inquirers seeking the truth. We are alienated from truth and are enemies of it. We are by nature idolaters, constructing images of truth shaped by our own desires. This was demonstrated once and for all when Truth became incarnate, present to us in the actual being and life of the man Jesus, and when our response to this Truth incarnate, a response including all the representatives of the best of human culture at that time and place, was to seek to destroy it.

It is this terrible reality that the liberal typically fails to recognize. It is absurd to say, as many do, that the traditional Christian teaching about the radical corruption of human nature comes from sources alien to the Jesus of the Gospels — St. Paul and St. Augustine being the prime suspects. This radical judgment on human nature is part of the very marrow of the New Testament witness. It would be strictly intolerable and therefore unbelievable if it were not seen through the eyes of those who have been brought to a new life by the resurrection of Jesus from the dead and by the gift of the Holy Spirit. Apart from this, the only possible implication of the death of Jesus would be the one enacted by Judas when he went out and hanged himself. It is possible, however, to avoid the implication set forth by Judas and to face and acknowledge the terrible reality exposed in the crucifixion of Jesus. This is evidenced by the fact that there *are* those who have been brought through the death and burial of the old self, that self which was confident in its own power to know the truth, and who have been incorporated into the life of him who is the truth and who is able to lead us into the truth. It is they alone who are truly free.

Because this is so, the witness that Christians bear to the truth must be a humble and penitent witness. This dying and being brought to life is something that must be continually renewed, reknown, and reenacted throughout life. The confession of the truth will be part of a continual indebtedness to grace. It will never be the kind of certainty which supposes that I can become a possessor of the truth by the exercise of my own natural powers. It will mean that my understanding of the truth must be constantly open to revision and correction, but — and this is the crucial point — *only* and *always* within the irreversible commitment to Jesus Christ. If that commitment is questioned, then I am once again a clueless wanderer in the darkness, bamboozled by the products of my own imagination. The strength of the liberal tradition is its willingness to be open to new truth. And the gospel itself makes this liberal mind possible; for if we know that Jesus is indeed the Word made flesh, the visible and knowable presence in the midst of history from whom and for whom all things exist, then we shall meet new experiences of any kind of reality with the confidence that we are given the clue for their understanding. But if that clue itself is questioned or abandoned, then we become clueless playthings of the winds and waves of fashion, "blown about by every wind of doctrine." Contemporary church life furnishes an abundance of illustrations.

The fundamentalist critique of liberal theology must be taken seriously. But fundamentalists do a disservice to the gospel when, as sometimes happens, they adopt a style of certainty more in the tradition of Descartes than in the truly evangelical spirit. This can show itself in several familiar ways. Sometimes it is an anxiety about the threat that new discoveries in science may pose to Christian faith — an anxiety that betrays a lack of total confidence in the central truth of the gospel that Jesus is the Word made flesh. Sometimes it leads to a refusal to reconsider long-held beliefs in the light of fresh reflection on the witness of Scripture. One may contrast this with the truly liberal spirit shown by the Jews of Berea, for when confronted by the revolutionary message of the apostle, they did not simply reject it but "examined the Scriptures every day to see if what Paul said was true" (Acts 17:11). And it can manifest itself in a claim for the objective truth of the Christian message that seems to depend on the acceptance of the false dualism of Enlightenment thought. Insofar as the word "objective" is used as a synonym for "really true," one must of course accept it unreservedly. But, it seems to me, its use in the context of modern thinking can lead to the false impression that the Christian faith is a matter of demonstrable fact rather than a matter of grace received in faith. Perhaps liberals would be more ready to listen to the very serious question put to them by fundamentalists if the latter were more manifestly speaking as those who must think, as they must live, as debtors to grace. There is much wisdom in the simple words with which Herbert Butterfield concluded his study of Christianity and history: "Hold to Christ, and for the rest be totally uncommitted."

One of the most quoted sayings of the Enlightenment was that of Lessing when he spoke of the "great, ugly ditch" which separates history from science. Accidental happenings of history, he said, cannot prove eternal truths of reason. The gospel is an account of events in history. "God so loved the world that he gave his only begotten Son. . . ." From the standpoint of the Enlightenment, this statement does not validate any claim to know eternal truths of reason. Any conclusions drawn from this historical statement would be subjective. One way of describing

71

what happened at the birth of the modern era is to say that there was a shift in the perception of reliable truth from a story (the story told in the Bible) to a model of reality in terms of timeless laws of nature. The paradigm for the latter was, as I have noted earlier, Newton's mathematical physics. Newton's model calls for no faith in alleged divine revelation. Its functioning can be grasped by normal human powers of observation and reason. If the functioning of the cosmos is to be understood by means of this model, since there is no way of discovering the purpose for which the cosmos exists simply by observation of its workings, it follows that we are free to impose our own purposes on the cosmos. And, furthermore, insofar as we understand the ways in which the cosmos functions, we shall be able to formulate laws of nature that will enable us to predict with certainty the outcome of the actions we take. But, in the absence of any reliable information about the purpose (if any) for which the cosmos exists, the purposes we impose upon it will be as diverse as the persons whose purposes they are.

If, by contrast, we look for reliable truth in a story, the position will be quite different. A story is constituted by the actions of people who make choices, choices which are never totally predictable. If we understand our lives in terms of a story, we know that things are not predictable. A story always has room for surprises. The Bible, taken as a whole in its canonical shape, tells the story of the cosmos and of the human race in terms of the activity of its Author and Governor. In the language of Hans Frei (*The Eclipse of Biblical Narrative*), the Bible renders the character of God. We only come to know the character of a person by learning the story of that person's life — how he or she speaks and acts in different situations. In the Bible as a whole, we are encountered by one whose character becomes clear as we continually allow the story to fill our minds. As we do this, we become aware that our lives are part of this universal story, and they are given a shape as part of it. We are given a sense of where we have come from and where we are going. This does not, however, provide us with means for the infallible prediction of what is to come; the Author has given us sufficient proof of his capacity for surprising us! But we have a confidence which is based on trust in him. Our lives are shaped, therefore, not by the confidence that we know enough of the laws of nature to chart our course with certainty, but by a faith (which can always be questioned) in the one whose story it is. I have affirmed that it is this biblical shaping that accounts for the distinctive character of the society we call Europe.

The Enlightenment, as I have suggested, was — from one point of view — a shift in the location of reliable truth from the story told in the Bible to the eternal truths of reason, of which the mathematical physics of Newton offered the supreme model. It was with confidence in the universal validity and reliability of these truths of reason that Europe reached out into the rest of the world with its civilizing mission. Even as recently as the 1930s, the famous Layman's Report *Rethinking Missions* saw the true function of the Christian missionary enterprise in terms of the universal communication of these eternal truths — the so-called "clear universals" which were valid for all human beings irrespective of their traditional cultures. I have referred to the dramatic collapse of this confidence and to the seminal figure of Nietzsche as the one who saw the inevitable outcome of the program of Enlightenment. Nietzsche and his disciples — the so-called postmodernists — have effectively turned Lessing on his head. The eternal truths of reason are in fact products of particular histories. Instead of eternal truths, we have *The Genealogy of Morals* (Nietzsche) and *The Archaeology Of the Social Sciences* (Michel Foucault). The self-evident truths of the Enlightenment are, we now see, not self-evident at all but only appear self-evident to a society which has been shaped by a particular story. (It is not self-evident to an orthodox Hindu that all individuals are born with equal rights to life, liberty, and the pursuit of happiness.) There are no timeless truths; there are only metanarratives which falsely claim to explain the human story as a whole but which are in fact themselves simply products of particular human histories.

Now it is obviously true that all our eternal truths and all our metanarratives are products of particular human histories. They are all socially and historically embodied. They do not exist in a suprahistorical, supracultural stratosphere. They are embodied in a particular language, using concepts, symbols, and models which have been developed in particular human communities. They are part of human culture, of particular human cultures. There is no reason to deny this.

But it is another matter if the conclusion is drawn that none of them are true or that their competing claims to account for reality are all equally true or (if you prefer the same thing in other words) equally false. That conclusion is unwarranted. It rests on the unstated assumption that truth must be something accessible apart from particular human languages, concepts, and models. The (true) assertion that all truth claims are culturally and historically embodied does not entail the (false) assertion that none of them makes contact with a reality beyond the human mind.

How, then, can we affirm the validity of these culturally and historically embodied truth claims? How can we be sure that these verbally formulated truth claims make contact with the realities of the minds which have formulated them? Plainly (as Thomas Torrance has pointed out), the relation between words and that which is not words cannot be stated in words. The relation is not a matter of verbal definition but of the total commitment of the whole person to that which is affirmed in the verbal statement.

Here we must refer again to that fatal step by which Descartes made the basis of certainty the thinking mind isolated from the whole embodied self and from the whole reality of which the human being is a part. There is no detached way of arriving at

74

objective truth, if this means a kind of truth claim not embodied in the affirmation of particular persons who use particular languages and concepts. I can only affirm the objectivity of a truth claim which I make by committing myself to live and act in accordance with this claim. If this is condemned as subjectivism and relativism, it is only because there lurks in the mind of the objector the illusion of a kind of knowledge which is not the knowledge of any human subject. The point can perhaps be sharpened by using two words which often play a part in discussion of these matters — the words "certain" and "fact."

For Descartes, as we have seen, the ideal of certainty was attained in mathematics. In the modern period, truth claims have been widely regarded as certain if they could be expressed in mathematical forms. This has been the ideal of scientific knowledge. But, as Einstein repeatedly said, the statements of mathematics are certain only when they make no contact with reality. As soon as a mathematical formula is applied to a situation in the world outside the mathematician's mind, it ceases to be certain. In Polanyi's summary, only statements that can be doubted make contact with reality. In other words, the mark of an indubitable statement is that it makes no contact with reality. If we are to make contact with reality, we must have the courage to make statements that can be doubted. There can be no knowing of reality without the courage to affirm what can be doubted and to act on that affirmation.

In addition to "certainty," the word "fact" also appears often in this discussion. Facts are supposed to be objective; interpretations of them, in contrast, are held to be subjective. That a man called Jesus was crucified and that it was alleged by his disciples that he had risen again — these are facts. That in this action God was reconciling the world to himself is interpretation, not fact, and is therefore subjective. But both statements are interpretations, the one being the interpretation of the disciples and the other being the interpretation shaped by the contemporary,

75

modern worldview. Facts are not entities that simply implant themselves in a vacant mind; they are grasped by a mind trained in a particular culture to grasp them. The same realities presented to a child of three and to a trained scientist will not be the same sort of facts to both of them. The latter's statement of the facts will he determined by his or her scientific training.

At the heart of the concern that drove Michael Polanyi into the field of philosophy was his recognition that scientific work involved the passionate, personal commitment of the scientist to a truth which is, in the beginning, only intuitively sensed but which can only be reached if there is a willingness to affirm belief in statements that can be doubted. The alternative would be the collapse into skepticism and nihilism that we are seeing all about us in the developed world.

The business of the church is to tell and to embody a story, the story of God's mighty acts in creation and redemption and of God's promises concerning what will be in the end. The church affirms the truth of this story by celebrating it, interpreting it, and enacting it in the life of the contemporary world. It has no other way of affirming its truth. If it supposes that its truth can be authenticated by reference to some allegedly more reliable truth claim, such as those offered by the philosophy of religion, then it has implicitly denied the truth by which it lives. In this sense, the church shares the postmodernists' replacement of eternal truths with a story. But there is a profound difference between the two. For the postmodernists, there are many stories, but no overarching truth by which they can be assessed. They are simply stories. The church's affirmation is that the story it tells, embodies, and enacts is the true story and that others are to be evaluated by reference to it.

The world, so far as recorded history enables us to know, has always been full of stories, myths which expressed in story form the way of understanding the human situation. Such myths do not claim factual truth, in the sense that their veracity can be checked against the record of contemporary witnesses or accessible artifacts. They express eternal truths in story form. By contrast, the story that the church tells is a competitor in the field where secular historians tell the story of a society, a nation, a civilization, or the story of the world. The church's story is not a different kind of story from the one these histories tell; its difference is with respect to the interpretation of the records which are the raw material common to them all. It is not a special kind of history isolated from the work of secular historians. It is, if you like, a counterhistory, interpreting the same evidence in a different way. Perhaps the point that I am making can be highlighted by observing that some theologians have affirmed that, while the crucifixion of Jesus is an event in history, the resurrection is not. Of course this drives a wedge right through the heart of the Christian creed. If, in fact, the tomb was not empty on that Sunday morning, then the crucifixion of Jesus has to be understood quite differently from the way it is to be understood if the tomb was empty. The church's affirmation is that the story it tells is the true interpretation of all human and cosmic history and that to understand history otherwise is to misunderstand it, therefore misunderstanding the human situation here and now.

This is a stupendous claim. It is rendered even more astounding when one considers the weakness, confusion, cowardice, and downright wickedness to be found in all generations in the body to which the telling of this story has been entrusted. There can be no attempt to hide the enormity of the gulf between the treasure entrusted to the church and the body to which this trust has been given, between the story that the church tells and the story of the church itself with its global span and long history. One must be quite honest about church history and about the church's present actions and attitudes.

Yet none of this is the last word. Here is where the demand to walk by faith is at its most urgent. In spite of the church's sin, God remains faithful to those whom he has called. The promise of the Holy Spirit's guidance has not been withdrawn. Even in the darkest hours, signs of the divine presence shine with a brightness that cannot be hidden. And the story that the church tells continues to exercise its power both to correct and reform the church and to convince and convert the world. And however grievous the apostasy of the church may be, it remains that God has entrusted to it this story and that there is no other body that will tell it. From age to age, the church lives under the authority of the story that the Bible tells, interpreted ever anew to new generations and new cultures by the continued leading of the Holy Spirit who alone makes possible the confession that Jesus is Savior and Lord. God's sovereignty is that of God's grace. It is as savior that God is Lord. It is as the one who overcomes our alienation from the truth that God reveals the truth. We are not, as we like to think, naturally lovers of the truth. It has become possible for us to know God and to speak confidently of God only because the beloved Son who knows the Father has taken our place in our estrangement from God and has made it possible to come to a true knowledge of God through him. So the revelation of God given to us in him is not a matter of coercive demonstration but of grace, of a love that forgives and invites. That reality of grace governs both the confidence we have in speaking of God and the manner in which we must commend the gospel to others.

But if we are to speak in these terms, we must deal in greater depth with the specific questions modernity and postmodernity raise concerning the authority of Scripture. In the discussion so far, I have simply taken this authority for granted. We cannot continue the discussion, however, without facing these questions, even if only briefly, and this must be the business of the next chapter.

6

Holy Scripture

I have said that the Enlightenment was, from one point of view,
a shift in the location of reliable truth from a story to a set
of eternal laws capable (in principle) of mathematical statement
and independent of accidental happenings in history. It was
inevitable that this shift should lead to a reevaluation of that
which had formerly been regarded as the locus of reliable truth
— namely, the Scriptures of the Old and New Testaments. These
could no longer be accepted as the final arbiter of truth. They
must be examined and evaluated like any other ancient scriptures. Of course, the change was not immediate. Scripture retained for a long time and still retains among many Christians
in the modern world an authority which sets it apart from other
ancient literature. But the shift was obviously unavoidable. These
ancient documents had to be assessed by the criteria developed
in modern scientific work if they were to have any authority at
all. Whatever might happen within the life of the church, the
scholarly world had to distinguish a scientific approach to the
Bible from the confessional approach of the churches. And as
training for the Christian ministry was assimilated to the critical
methods of modernity, thousands of prospective ordinands in
their earliest months of theological training had to be gently but
firmly moved from the confessional position to the scientific
one. What came to be known as the "historical-critical method"

grew to eventually be accepted as the only proper method for interpreting these ancient writings.

In the light of the argument of this essay so far, it is not necessary to argue the point that this move is misunderstood if it is seen as a move to a more objective understanding of the Bible. It is a move from one confessional stance to another, a move from one creed to another. But it is very hard to persuade the practitioners of the historical-critical method to recognize the creedal character of their approach. It will therefore be useful to refer to the clear enunciation given by Ernest Troeltsch in 1898 to the principles that should govern biblical interpretation:*

1. The principle of critical or methodological doubt: since any conclusion is subject to revision, historical inquiry can never achieve absolute certainty but only relative degrees of probability.

2. The principle of analogy: historical knowledge is possible because all events are similar in principle. We must assume that the laws of nature in biblical times were the same as now. Troeltsch refers to this as "the almighty power of analogy."

3. The principle of correlation: the phenomena of history are interrelated and interdependent, and no event can be isolated from the sequence of historical causes and effects.

It is helpful to have these principles set out in this way, and when this is done it immediately becomes obvious that this is a creedal position. These principles are assumed to be true in advance of anything that one might learn from the Bible. Clearly none of them can be demonstrated as matters of certainty. They are not called prejudices because, unlike prejudices, they are assumptions picked up from the plausibility structure that controls the world of modernity. It is worth looking at these three principles in turn and more closely:

(1) The principle of critical or methodological doubt is

---

* I owe this reference to an article by John D. Levenson in *First Things* (New York), February 1993. The summary of Troeltsch's list is done by John J. Collins.

already familiar as the kingpin of the Cartesian method. We have looked at the impasse into which it has led modernity, and there is no need to repeat the story. To put it in one sentence, the biblical story is here judged by a criterion which is inoperable — inoperable because the idea that we can have a certainty not open to doubt is an illusion.

(2) The principle of analogy can be stated in a *negative* form as follows: there can be no event that is unique. Quite obviously, this proposition is strictly impossible to prove. It is an easy victim of the principle of methodological doubt. It is, of course, possible to believe that nothing unique has ever happened or could ever happen, but it can never be more than an assumption. The assertion (which Christians make) that something unique has happened can of course be doubted, but it cannot be dismissed as an impossibility. And there are two things which might be said to justify at least the keeping of an open mind. The first is this: there is no analogy known by secular historians for the creation of the world. However we think about the beginning of all things, about the transition from nothingness to something, it is not an event which can be listed in a catalogue of similar events. The Christian tradition, on the other hand, claims that there *is* one event which is genuinely analogous — namely, the event of the incarnation. Christian tradition speaks of this as the beginning of a new creation, for there is indeed no other appropriate analogy. It is, of course, perfectly possible to disbelieve this. It is possible and indeed natural to think that cosmic and human existence is bound by eternal laws which can never change, that there can never be anything radically new, and that as things have been they forever will be. This is possible, natural, and very common. But there is no logical necessity requiring us to believe these positions and to thus disbelieve the Christian analogy of a new creation.

The second reason for pausing before accepting the almighty power of analogy as the ultimate reality of the universe is this:

Christians of all persuasions pray, "Your kingdom come." What are we, as Christians, asking for when we so pray? We already believe that God is the Supreme Ruler. If, nevertheless, we pray for God's kingly rule to come, then we are asking for something different from the present state of affairs. We are, surely, rejecting and rebelling against the almighty power of analogy. We are looking for something new, radically new. If, however, there can never be within history something radically new, what is the point of this prayer? In truth, of course, we are emboldened to pray this prayer, to make this unreasonable petition, because we believe that in Jesus this kingly rule has in fact broken into our history in an event which is without analogy except the analogy of creation and the analogy of the final consummation of all things. Apart from these unique events, for which there are no other analogies, the petition would surely be a mere aspiration without justification in the experience of human history.

(3) The principle of correlation affirms that all historical events are part of an unbroken nexus of cause-effect relationships. Here we seem to have a simple example of the reductionism I referred to during the discussion of Polanyi's hierarchy of levels of explanation. Certainly all happenings in history are part of a nexus of cause-effect relationships which can be explored at various levels. But this does not exclude the possibility that they may embody a purpose that is *not* exhaustively explained by tracing these relationships. Just as the physical structure of our bodies, explicable at various levels (atomic, molecular, mechanical, electrical, and so forth) does not prevent but makes possible the free exercise of our will in performing bodily acts; so — we must surely believe — the physical structure of the cosmos does not prevent God from effecting his will in the events of history. No doubt "all causes are adequate to the effects which they produce," but that does not mean that they can be totally explained in terms of their causes.

All of these three principles are easily recognizable as elements in the creed of modernity. We have noted the signs of the collapse of this creed and should perhaps also note that some biblical scholars find it hard to come to terms with the fact that their worldview is collapsing around them, even though they can still earn from the media the title of "radical" if they stick to this creed. But others have come to terms with the postmodernist development of modernism. As we have seen, it is characteristic of the postmodernists, following Nietzsche, that they do not expect answers in the form of eternal truths. They practice rather the "hermeneutic of suspicion" which leads the student of an ancient record to ask not What is the truth which is here articulated? but What is the interest which is here being advanced? The biblical material is thus interpreted in terms of the various power struggles in Israel and in the church. For example, a passage in the Old Testament is really an assertion of the claims of the northern kingdom against those of Judah or of the kingship against democratic forces. In the New Testament, the pastoral epistles are an attempt to assert the authority of the developing episcopate against the more prophetic and charismatic traditions of the early church. These are not the only examples; there are numerous others.

It is, of course, idle to try to refute these proposals by means of rational arguments appealing to more fundamental truths. The materialist interpretation with its "hermeneutic of suspicion" is itself a denial of the existence of such rational arguments or such fundamental truths. Perhaps the only possible way to respond to this kind of biblical interpretation is to point out that it is very easy to deconstruct the whole argument by employing its own methods. The materialist interpretation of the Bible must, on these principles, be regarded not as the unveiling of any truth, but as a concealed effort (rather successful so far) to assert the authority of academics over ecclesiastics. Perhaps one good fruit of this method might be that pastors and preachers have become less timid in dealing with the pronouncements of academics!

The practice of the historical-critical method, in spite of the useful results it has produced in our understanding of the ways in which the biblical material was formed, is nevertheless full of self-contradictions. Before proceeding to attempt a more positive statement about biblical authority, I will mention two of these self-contradictions.

It is a commonly expressed view among biblical scholars that, because all the biblical material is the product of particular times, places, and cultures, its truth claim cannot be absolute. All truth claims are relativized by their origin in particular cultural settings. But the historical-critical method is itself the product of a particular culture, and we have discussed the ways in which this culture was formed and the forces which now threaten it with collapse. The historical-critical method therefore must be applied to itself.

When the critic rejects the traditional Christian view of the Bible as the authoritative communication of God's acts in creation and redemption on the ground that it is a confessional rather than an objective interpretation, one has to ask for the justification of the critical enterprise itself. The biblical material contains only a minute fraction of all the material available to us from the ancient world. Why, then, are such disproportionate resources devoted to its study? Why do universities all over the world have large departments devoted to the study of the biblical documents, while the whole of the rest of ancient literature from all the ancient civilizations of the six continents has no comparable attention paid to it? The reason is obvious: it is because the Bible is the sacred Scripture of the largest faith community occupying this planet. It is only because the Bible is Holy Scripture for a large part of the world's total population that it is an object of special attention. Is it not odd that, for the purpose of scholarly study, the very reason for which it is studied should be set aside as unscientific? Interpreters of the Bible are often heard appealing to the "overwhelming majority of scholars" as grounds for setting aside the views of those who read the Bible within the faith commitments of the biblical writers themselves. If we take a global view and a long view, must we not say that the opinion of a very small minority in a culture that appears to be collapsing is asserting an authority that fits oddly with their real situation?

These two points are of minor importance. Majorities are not necessarily right. I make them only to draw attention to what seem to be self-contradictions in the defenses sometimes offered by the historical critics. I now turn to look briefly at one attempt to resist that erosion of traditional faith that has been brought about by the work of biblical criticism. Protestant fundamentalism is, like liberalism, a child of the Enlightenment. It has sought to reassert the authority of the Bible in the new situation created by modernity. The concern was right, but the method was wrong. I am referring to a kind of fundamentalism which seeks to affirm the factual, objective truth of every statement in the Bible and which thinks that if any single factual error were to be admitted, biblical authority would collapse. Human judgment would replace the word of God. The unavoidable existence of discrepancies in matters of fact to be found in the Bible was sometimes countered by the statement that the original text (now lost) was without error. In other words, the possibility of error was admitted in the long history of the transmission of the text from, say Isaiah, to a student in the twentieth century, but these errors only occurred at a date some time after the (unknown) moment at which the original Hebrew text was written.

This leads to absurdity and arises from a false concept of biblical authority imposed on the Bible by minds shaped by the Enlightenment. Once again we are dealing with concepts of objectivity, of facts, and of certainty which are typical of minds shaped by modernity. We have to be grateful to the scholars of the historical-critical period for doing so much to disentangle the various strands in the biblical material and to throw light on the ways by which each of its parts took shape in a long tradition, both oral and written. At every point in the story of the transmission of biblical material from the original text to today we are dealing with the interaction of men and women with God. At every point, human judgment and human fallibility are involved, as they are involved in every attempt we make today to act faithfully in new situations. The idea that at a certain point in this long story a line was drawn before which everything is divine word and after which everything is human judgment is absurd. I have every sympathy with the fundamentalist's rejection of scholarship that denies any real authority to Scripture, but I cannot accept a kind of defense of the Bible that rests on a surrender to the very forces threatening to destroy biblical authority. But the theological liberal, who is upset when he hears the Bible referred to as the word of God, is likewise led astray by allowing alien norms to control his judgment. The liberal's disapproval of this way of describing the Bible presupposes some beliefs about what it would mean to speak of anything as the word of God. One has to ask what these beliefs are and where they come from. Such a probing will always lead to some kind of faith commitment that is open to doubt.

Let me go back to the point made at the beginning of this essay, namely, that the launching of the Christian story into the life of the classical world of antiquity eventually required a whole new starting point for thought. The Christian story could not fit into and be judged by the assumptions that controlled classical thought. It had to be recognized as itself a new starting point for thought. By the same token, we have to recognize that we must allow the Bible to provide us with its own account of what it means to speak of the word of God. We have to learn by the actual practice of living with the Bible how and in what ways God speaks. In the words of the Prayer Book collect, we have to hear, read, mark, and learn and inwardly digest the Bible, taking it wholly into ourselves in a way that shapes the very substance of our thinking and feeling and doing. It is less important to ask a Christian what he or she believes about the Bible than it is to inquire what he or she does with it.

Christian discipleship, like all human activity, is embedded in a tradition and cannot live apart from that tradition. Traditions consist of memories cherished in oral or written form and shared practices and rituals. These memories and practices are the memories and practices of a community and have to be understood in the context of its life. For the Christian tradition the supremely authoritative memory is that embodied in the Bible, and the supremely authoritative practices are the sacraments of baptism and the eucharist. These together define what Christianity is and, conversely, are rightly understood only in the context of the Christian tradition. The ways in which people are drawn into the Christian tradition are enormously various but always include living contact with members of the Christian community. At some point, the new disciple is introduced to the Bible and learns to know it as an integral part of the church's liturgy and (if the new disciple is literate) as something for private reading. It embodies the story that shapes and interprets the community. Of course, the new disciple's reading will be shaped by his or her previous culture. If, for example, the new disciple is a Tamil and the Bible he reads is in Tamil, all the key words will initially have the meaning that they have in the mainly Hindu Tamil culture. Only slowly, as the movement of the story unfolds, will the reader discover that old assumptions have to be revised.

The reading of the Bible must therefore necessarily be a critical activity. Old beliefs are called into question. Moreover, the variety of the biblical material demands critical activity. How is the ferocity of Joshua's campaign to be reconciled with the Sermon on the Mount? How is the exclusiveness of Ezra and Nehemiah to be reconciled with the universalism of Ruth and Jonah? How do we relate Paul's description of the Roman power as God's servant (Rom. 13) with the identification of the same power with the work of Satan in Revelation? Which of these is the word of God? There is no chance of the critical faculty of any serious reader of the Bible being put to sleep. But, as always, the essential question is this: on the basis of what assumptions are the critical questions being asked? From within the Christian tradition, the answer to that question is that the critical questions are asked on the basis of the fact that the word of God is Jesus Christ. On this basis, the reading of the Bible involves a continual twofold movement: we have to understand Jesus in the context of the whole story, and we have to understand the whole story in the light of Jesus.

On the one hand, we cannot understand Jesus except in the context of the Bible as a whole. To detach Jesus from this story is to create a mythical figure. In his teaching and in his actions he speaks and acts as one who brings the story of God's dealing with Israel to its point of crisis and decision. And the apostolic preaching is not the announcement of a new religion but the announcement that the God of Israel has now fulfilled his promises and declared his whole purpose for all the nations.

If we do not know the whole story and context of Jesus, then we cannot truly know him and thus cannot truly know God the Father. We need to see this God of Israel both in his wrath and his infinite mercy. We need to learn a holiness that rejects all compromise with evil and a generosity that seeks and saves the lost. We need to learn to know God as he is. There is no way by which we come to know a person except by dwelling in his or her story and, in the measure that may be possible, becoming part of it. The person who allows the biblical story to be the all-surrounding ambience of daily life and who continually seeks to place all experiences in this context finds that daily life is a continuous conversation with the one whose character is revealed in the biblical story taken as a whole. There is a world of difference between this and a concept of God developed out of reflection on life's experience apart from this story. As we live with the tension between the awesome holiness of God and his limitless kindness and as we bring this tension always to the person of Jesus himself in whom these seeming opposites are held together in a single life and death of judgment and mercy, we are led into a knowledge of God. To be more precise, we are enabled in growing measure to be admitted into that intimacy that Jesus had with his Father, an intimacy he spoke of when he said that no one knows the Father except the Son and those to whom the Son makes him known (Luke 10:22).

So, on the one hand, if we are to understand Jesus rightly, we need the whole story. On the other hand, we have to read the whole story from Genesis onward as having its true interpretation in the total fact of the incarnation — the birth, ministry, death, resurrection, and glory of Jesus. For our whole understanding of what it means to speak of the Bible as the word of God, it is absolutely essential to hold in mind that way in which Jesus communicated his knowledge of the Father. The manner in which Jesus makes the Father known is not in infallible, unrevisable, irreformable statements. He did not write a book which would have served forever as the unquestionable and irreformable statement of the truth about God. He formed a community of friends and shared his life with them. He left it to them to be his witnesses, and — as we know — their witness has come to us in varied forms; we know about very few of the words and deeds of Jesus with the kind of certainty Descartes identified with reliable knowledge. To wish that it were otherwise is to depart from the manner in which God has chosen to make himself known. The doctrine of verbal inerrancy is a direct denial of the way in which God has chosen to make himself known to us as the Father of our Lord Jesus Christ. And, if Jesus is indeed the Word made flesh and therefore the one through whom we are to understand God's dealings with Israel, then we must conclude that God's way of dealing with Israel was not otherwise.

Jesus promised his disciples that they would receive the gift of the Holy Spirit, the Spirit of the Father and of the Son, and that the Spirit would interpret to them the meaning of his words and deeds and lead them into the truth as a whole. That promise was fulfilled. This gift of the Spirit, however, did not make the disciples infallible any more than the same gift given to the prophetic writers of the Old Testament made them infallible. Again, at the risk of wearisome repetition, we must guard against the imposition on the Scriptures of the dichotomy between objective and subjective ways of knowing. We are *not* required to choose between two alternative ways of understanding Scripture: either an objective account of the deeds and words of God or a subjective record of the religious experience of the writers. The prophets and apostles of the Old and New Testaments belonged to the same world as we do, a world in which knowing is a matter of the commitment of personal subjects to the clearest possible understanding of the reality of which we are a part. The church has defined the boundaries of Scripture as canonical and thus as having a position of decisive authority within the entire ongoing tradition, but that does not mean that the conditions governing all human knowing of God do not apply within the biblical canon.

In the course of those discourses in which Jesus, according to the Fourth Gospel, prepared the disciples for what was to come, he said to them, "I no longer call you servants, for a servant does not know his master's business. Instead, I have called you friends, for everything that I have learned from my Father I have made known to you" (John 15:15). This is the clearest indication of the nature of Scriptural authority. The truth is not imposed upon us, for indeed truth has not done its work unless and until we have learned to honor and love it from our hearts as truth. But we do not reach truth unless we allow ourselves to be exposed to and drawn by a truth which is beyond our present understanding. What was said about the nature of scientific discovery is relevant here. The important thing is not how we formulate a doctrine of biblical authority but how we allow the Bible to function in our daily lives. We grow into a knowledge of God by allowing the biblical story to awaken our imagination and to challenge and stimulate our thinking and acting. What we cannot yet understand or accept must nevertheless be allowed to challenge us to more daring thought and commitment. The apophatic tradition in the life of the church is a valid warning to us against supposing that we have all the mystery of the Godhead captured in our theology. We are compelled over and over again, as we allow the story to shape our minds, to exclaim with St. Paul, "Oh, the depth of the riches of the wisdom and knowledge of God! How unsearchable his judgments, and his paths beyond tracing out!" (Rom. 11:33). But — and this is the important point — this sense of the ineffable mystery of God does not arise out of metaphysical speculation about the vastness of things; it arises from the contemplation of the story of God's dealing with his people. The mystery is not so much a metaphysical one as a moral one. It is the mystery of a holiness that can yet embrace the unholy. It is the mystery of the divine love for the unlovely. It is the mystery of grace.

We are, in the long run, shaped by what we attend to. In very many respects, we are not our own masters or mistresses. Events beyond our control impinge upon us all the time. But in one respect we are free: we are free to determine what we will attend to. If we allow the Bible to be that which we attend to above all else, we will be saved from two dangers: The first is the danger of the closed mind. The Bible leaves an enormous space open for exploration. If our central commitment is to Jesus, who is the Word of God incarnate in our history, we shall know that in following him we have the clue to the true understanding of all that is, seen and unseen, known and yet to be discovered. We shall therefore be confident explorers. The second is the danger of the mind open at both ends, the mind which is prepared to entertain anything but has a firm hold of nothing. We shall be saved from the clueless wandering which sometimes takes to itself the name of pilgrimage. A pilgrim is one who turns his back on some familiar things and sets his face in the direction of the desired goal. The Christian is called to be a pilgrim, a learner to the end of her days. But she knows the Way.

7

Through Faith Alone

I am writing this book as a missionary who is concerned to
commend the truth of the gospel in a culture that has sought
for absolute certainty as the ideal of true knowledge but now
despairs of the possibility of knowing truth at all, a culture that
therefore responds to the Christian story by asking, "But how
can we know that it is true?" There is a long tradition of Christian
theology that goes under the name "apologetics" and that seeks
to respond to this question and to demonstrate the "reasonableness of Christianity." The assumption often underlying titles of
this kind is that the gospel can be made acceptable by showing
that it does not contravene the requirements of reason as we
understand them within the contemporary plausibility structure.
The heart of my argument is that this is a mistaken policy. The
story the church is commissioned to tell, if it is true, is bound
to call into question any plausibility structure which is founded
on other assumptions. The affirmation that the One by whom
and through whom and for whom all creation exists is to be
identified with a man who was crucified and rose bodily from
the dead cannot possibly be accommodated within any plausibility structure except one of which it is the cornerstone. In any
other place in the structure it can only be a stone of stumbling.
The reasonableness of Christianity will be demonstrated (insofar
as it can be) not by adjusting its claims to the requirements of

a preexisting structure of thought but by showing how it can provide an alternative foundation for a different structure. The title of one of the most famous writings of the Enlightenment was *Religion within the Limits of Reason*. The American philosopher Wolterstorff has reversed the title with his book *Reason within the Limits of Religion*. The reversal of words is justified if one remembers that all human reasoning is embodied in a specific culture and that, through most of human history, religion has been the most powerful factor in the shaping of culture. To look outside of the gospel for a starting point for the demonstration of the reasonableness of the gospel is itself a contradiction of the gospel, for it implies that we look for the *logos* elsewhere than in Jesus.

The obvious implication of this argument, therefore, is that the proper form of apologetics is the preaching of the gospel itself and the demonstration — which is not merely or primarily a matter of words — that it does provide the best foundation for a way of grasping and dealing with the mystery of our existence in this universe. Needless to say, this demonstration can never be more than partial and tentative. It is, according to the gospel, only on the day of judgment that the demonstration will be complete and decisive. Until then, my commitment to the truth of the gospel is a commitment of faith. If I am further pressed to justify this commitment (as I have often been), my only response has to be a personal confession. The story is not my construction. In ways that I cannot fully understand but always through the witness of those who went before me in the company of those called to be witnesses, I have been laid hold of and charged with the responsibility of telling this story. I am only a witness, not the Judge who alone can give the final verdict. But as a witness I am under obligation — the obligation of a debtor to the grace of God in Jesus Christ — to give my witness. I cannot pretend to anticipate the final judgment by offering any proof other than the fact that my life is committed to the truth of this witness.

In my own experience, I find that this position is questioned from three sides: from the Catholic tradition of natural theology, from Protestant fundamentalism, and from liberal theology of all kinds. At the risk of going over ground already partially covered, it may be helpful to look at these three criticisms in order:

The first critical standpoint comes from the long tradition of natural theology. From this standpoint, the stance I have suggested is attacked as being an abandonment of the responsible use of reason. It is a blind leap in the dark. It requires more rational justification. How, it is asked, am I to believe that Jesus is the Word of God if I do not have rational grounds for believing that the word "God" stands for any actual reality?

In reply to this, four points are in order:

1. We are not speaking of a blind leap into darkness but of a personal response to a personal calling. When Jesus called the first disciples with the words: "Follow me," he was certainly calling for an act of faith. He did not offer any demonstrable certainties. And so it is with everyone who has been so called through the faithfulness of the first apostles and their successors. To regard this as cognitively inferior to the rational demonstration of supposedly certain truths is to assume that the ultimate reality with which we have to deal is not personal but impersonal. In the investigation of impersonal realities we may ask for the kind of indubitable certainties that the Age of Reason demanded, even though subsequent history has shown that they are not attainable. But if the ultimate reality with which, or rather with whom, we have to deal is the being of the triune God, then the response of personal faith to a personal calling is the only way of knowing that reality. To rule this out as unreasonable is to make an *a priori* decision against the possibility that ultimate reality is personal.

2. The objection from natural theology also seems to rest on the assumption that there is available a kind of knowledge

95

which does not rest on any faith commitment. It denies the truth of Augustine's slogan, "I believe in order to know." I have already argued that this setting of reason against faith is absurd. Reason is not an independent means for finding out what is the case. It is not a substitute for information. In order to be informed, we have to make acts of trust in the traditions we have inherited and in the evidence of our senses. Moreover, as has already been said, all systematic reasoning has to begin by taking for granted certain things that are accepted without argument. There must be data without argument or, at least, without prior demonstration. I have already referred to the argument of Roy Clouser in his book *The Myth of Religious Neutrality*. There exists no neutral reason that can decide impartially on the truth or falsehood of the Christian gospel. On the contrary, if it is true that Jesus *is* the Word made flesh, then to know Jesus must be the basis for all true knowledge. We therefore have to recognize that the ancient words "The fear of the Lord is the beginning of wisdom" has a wider range of reference than is often supposed.

3. Having said this, it is now important to add that it follows from the above argument that there is a proper kind of theology that deals with the area natural theology addresses. If one may put it so, it covers the same field but starts from the other end. It does not start from somewhere outside the gospel in order to demonstrate the truth of the gospel but starts from the gospel itself, seeking to show how this starting point illuminates all our other experience. This is a true and necessary form of apologetics. In preaching the gospel, it is our business to show, insofar as our knowledge and experience equip us to do so, how the Christian story enables us to understand and deal with the whole range of human experience in both public and private life. Once again we follow the path suggested in Augustine's slogan: we believe in order to understand. We do not argue from experience to the gospel. On the contrary, it is the gospel accepted in faith which enables us to experience all reality in a new way and to find that all reality does indeed reflect the glory of God.

4. The points made in the three preceding paragraphs refer to the role of natural theology in Christian apologetics. There is, of course, a long pre-Christian tradition of natural theology. If, as for most of the great thinkers of classical antiquity, alleged divine revelation is not a reliable source of certain truth or if we disallow the Christian claims regarding God's revelation of himself in Jesus Christ, then natural theology is surely a perfectly legitimate enterprise. But for those who have become believers in the gospel of the Word made flesh, there is something improper, as I have argued, in supposing that this faith can be validated by the arguments of natural theology. This has special poignancy if we remember, as we must always remember, that when we speak of God's self-revelation in Christ, we are speaking of an immeasurably costly act of self-giving for our redemption and reconciliation. When we know that God has done this infinitely gracious thing, is it not inappropriate for us to respond, to put it crudely, "Thank you, but I have other collateral sources of information"? The truth surely is not that we come to know God by reasoning from our unredeemed experience but that what God has done for us in Christ gives us the eyes through which we can begin to truly understand our experience in the world.

In addition to the attack from natural theology, there is a second attack. It comes from what I have called Protestant fundamentalism. I hesitate to use the word "fundamentalism," since it has become common to label anyone who firmly believes in the truth of his or her religion a fundamentalist. In this sense, I am myself happy to be called a fundamentalist. But I am referring to something more specific. I have argued (in agreement with the postmodernists) that all truth claims are culturally and historically embodied. The Christian gospel arises out of the culture of one people among all the peoples of the world, the

people of Israel. The claim, of course, is that within this particular culture there was present, in the man Jesus, the eternal
Word through whom and for whom all things exist. But those
who make this claim do not occupy a position above other
particular cultures or histories. I have found myself attacked at
this point on the ground that this is a surrender to subjectivity.
The safety of the church and of the Christian confession requires,
it is said, that we affirm the "objective" truth of what the gospel
affirms. If the word "objective" here means "really true," then I
am happy. But the claim is made that we must affirm the factual
truth of every statement in the Bible as a matter of indubitable
certainty and that, if this position is surrendered, we are in a
world of subjectivity and relativism along with the rest of contemporary society. I have been told that there are context-independent criteria of truth on the basis of which one can undertake
to demonstrate the truth of the gospel.

One can understand this anxiety that the gospel should not
be allowed to sink into the swamp of relativism where there are
no firm footholds, and what is true for you may not be true for
me. But this way of defending the truth of the gospel will not
work. Two things can be said in reply to the fundamentalist
stance:

1. In seeking a kind of supracultural and indubitable certainty, these Christians have fallen into the trap set by Descartes.
They are seeking a kind of certainty that does not acknowledge
the certainty of faith as the only kind of certainty available. The
only one who has a context-independent standpoint is God. The
fundamental error of Descartes, surely, was the supposition that
we ourselves can have such a standpoint. Christian faith is not
a matter of logically demonstrable certainties but of the total
commitment of fallible human beings putting their trust in the
faithful God who has called them. I believe and trust that the
Bible is the true rendering of the story of God's acts in creation
and redemption and therefore the true rendering of the character

of God. At the core of the biblical story, there is a record of events in history. The biblical accounts of the beginning and the end of the world are, however, obviously not of the kind of accounts which rest upon indubitable Cartesian certainty, since no human evidence is available. The stories of the beginning are reshapings of the contemporary, available cosmologies to reflect that knowledge of God's ways and purposes that had been given to the prophets of Israel by God. Likewise, the vision of the end of the world in the last book of the Bible uses the images that Israel and the church had learned to use through their experience of God's dealing with them, his people. It is a confusion of categories to use the constantly changing modern views of cosmology to call into question the unchanging truth about God and his relation to the world and human life, a truth embodied in the protology and eschatology of the Bible.

The heart of the Christian faith from the first apostles onward has been that the story told in the Bible is the true story of God's dealings with the people he had chosen to be the bearers of his purpose for the world, and that those through whom the story has come down to us were enabled by his Holy Spirit — the same Spirit by whom Jesus was anointed and empowered — to interpret truly his dealings with his people. But the Bible is also the work of sinful and fallible human beings whose sins had to be constantly rebuked and whose misunderstandings had to be corrected. The very heart of the Bible is in this long, patient wrestling of God with a sinful and fallible people. The writer of the letter to the Hebrews summarizes the whole story as the story of a faith that grasps what cannot yet be seen, and he calls upon his readers to exercise the same faith. To convert the Bible into a compendium of indubitably certain facts is to impose upon it a character alien to itself, a character that is the typical product of minds shaped by the Enlightenment.

2. This way of understanding the Bible can and does often lead to a kind of hard rationalism that is remote from grace.

Christian discipleship is a kind of life lived by faith in the grace of God. The arrogance of supposedly indubitable certainties is uncongenial to it. Indubitable certainties call for the submission of the intellect even if the heart is unpersuaded. (And indubitable certainties, as we have been reminded, make no contact with reality.) But the gospel is not a matter of indubitable certainties; it is the offer of a grace that can only be accepted in faith, a faith in which both heart and intellect join.

In addition to being criticized by natural theology and Protestant fundamentalism, the position I am seeking to establish comes under attack from a third tradition: theological liberalism. The assertion that the biblical story, with its crucial turning point being the events concerning Jesus, must be accepted in faith as the starting point for all our thinking — such an assertion is unacceptable dogmatism in the eyes of many in the liberal tradition. And it is fundamental to the liberal tradition that all such dogma must be open to critical evaluation. Clearly, anyone who claims the name "Christian" has to take the Bible, or at least the New Testament, very seriously. But in the liberal tradition, the Bible cannot have the kind of ultimate authority I have suggested. It is, after all, the product of human experience; and, like all records of human experience, it must be tested in the light of the wider experience of the human race. It must take its place along with other records of human religious experience and be subject to the same kind of critical questioning as are the others. Liberals will, therefore, gladly acknowledge that God may speak to the human mind and conscience through the Bible, but they are uncomfortable with any identification of the Bible as the word of God.

The great value of the liberal tradition is its readiness to listen to new truth and to be open to questioning. There are many times when one has to be thankful for this, in contrast to the kind of dogmatism incapable of hearing anything that calls present beliefs into question. Precisely because it concerns our whole being and destiny, religious belief can be so tightly held that the mind is closed to anything new. Against this, the liberal tradition is a refreshing protest. But theological liberalism can itself become a dogmatic position that is closed to the witness of the gospel. The principle that every dogma must be open to question is itself a dogma open to question. I suggest four lines along which questions should be raised against the central dogma of theological liberalism:

1. Liberalism has accepted the critical principle of Descartes and his successors as an integral part of its method. In the preceding pages, I have tried to show how this inevitably leads to nihilism. All grasping of the truth concerning the world beyond our consciousness is the work of minds shaped by a tradition that uses a language and a set of concepts and models developed over many generations. The historical-critical method upon which liberal theologians rely in their use of Scripture is one part of such a tradition. Those who are shaped by this tradition work with certain, quite specific presuppositions, which I have discussed in a previous chapter. These presuppositions are so much a part of the reigning plausibility structure of contemporary modern society that it is hard for those who accept them to recognize that these presuppositions are only a few among a whole possible set of presuppositions, and that there are no rational grounds on which it could be shown that they have a superior epistemological status to the presuppositions that a Christian (or Jewish) reader brings to the Scriptures. They form part of a particular cultural tradition that has had a relatively short life, showing many signs of disintegration.

In contrast to the liberal reader of the Bible, who stands within the tradition of the historical-critical principle, the confessional reader stands within the tradition of the Christian church. The presuppositions here are those of the gospel itself, namely, that in Jesus the Word of God was made flesh, lived a human life, died for the sin of the world, and rose again. These presuppositions govern Christians' reading. They read as members of that same community whose story is told in the Bible. It is that community that has put the Bible into their hands and has taught them how to understand it. They read as believers. The difference between this way of reading the Bible and the historical-critical way is not that the latter is neutral or scientific whereas the former is confessional or sectarian; rather, it is the difference between two confessions, two traditions of interpretation developed in two different human communities. From the perspective of the much longer and wider experience of the Christian church, the historical-critical approach to the Bible is part of a cultural movement that has been fruitful in many respects but that is now in the process of disintegration. From a Christian point of view, there is something naive about the confidence of liberal theologians who suppose that the critical method provides a standpoint more secure than that offered by the historical faith of the universal church.

2. The principle that every dogma must be open to question runs into the difficulty that, in human affairs, action is required before all questions can be asked and answered. In his famous essay *The Will to Believe,* William James gives us a parable that illustrates the point I am making: A man climbing a cliff finds his hold slipping. Close by there is a tree growing out of a cleft in the rock. If he transfers himself to the tree, will it hold his weight? There is no way of deciding the matter in advance of action. There is no possibility of keeping an open mind. The climber has to make a decision on the evidence available, and that will be the final decision. The proposition that every dogma must be open to question is a typical product of that separation of thought from action, which we have traced to Descartes. We are continually required to act on beliefs that are not demonstrably certain and to commit our lives to propositions that can be doubted. The liberal who discounts the Christian interpretation of the biblical narrative on the ground that its truth cannot be demonstrated continues nevertheless to act on other beliefs whose truth cannot be demonstrated but are accepted anyway because they are part of the plausibility structure. Since the birth of the church, it has never been a secret that the acceptance of the full truth of the gospel announcement — that in the events concerning Jesus, God was himself performing those acts that are determinative for the history of the world — meant a radical questioning of the presuppositions of the majority of humankind. To decline the evangelical invitation to do exactly that is not to have the security of objective truth as opposed to confessional prejudice. It is to have chosen another confession.

3. Liberal theologians speak much of experience and frequently describe the Bible as particular record of human religious experience. But experience can be of many kinds, and we have to make distinctions. The experience of having a stomachache does not provide us with any information about a world of realities beyond the sufferer — only perhaps something about the eating habits of the person concerned. But the experience of seeing a great work of art does tell us something about a world beyond ourselves. Of course the Bible describes human experiences, but it does not speak of them in those terms; it speaks of the mighty acts of God. Of course these acts are understood and made part of the reader's awareness through the experience of human beings who were witnesses of them. But their witness concerns what God has done and not just what they have felt. And if God did indeed do the things of which the gospel speaks, then these accounts of them cannot be filed away in a catalogue of the varieties of religious experience. The story must either be disbelieved or it must become the fundamental presupposition of all our thought and action.

4. But perhaps the fundamental flaw in the tradition of theological liberalism lies at the point of its most attractive feature. The liberal mind is at its best in challenging us to be open to new truth, to be fearless in exploring all reality, and to be humble in recognizing the vastness and mystery that we try to comprehend with our finite minds. But even the language about the greatness and the unfathomable depths of the mystery of God can be the cloak for a calamitous error. The error is the supposition that it is we who are the explorers, that the real questions are the ones we formulate and put to the universe, and that our minds have a sovereign freedom to explore a reality waiting to be discovered. Our peril is that, out of the vastness of the unplumbed mystery, we summon up images that are the creations of our own minds. The human heart, as Calvin said, is a factory of idols.

The gospel challenges liberals' thinking in the sharpest possible way, and perhaps this is the hardest thing for them to accept. It exposes as illusion the liberal picture — the picture of ourselves as sovereign explorers who formulate the real questions in a search for a yet-to-be-discovered reality. The gospel undermines our questions with a question that comes to us from the mystery we thought to explore. It is a question as piercing and shattering as the voice that spoke to Job out of the whirlwind. It exposes our false pretensions. We are *not* honest and open-minded explorers of reality; we are alienated from reality because we have made ourselves the center of the universe. Before we continue with our questions, we have to answer a question put to us from the heart of the mystery. We have to answer that anguished question, "Adam, where are you?" We have to learn that we are lost and that we have to be rescued. We have to answer the call of the one who has come to rescue us and learn that it is only in him and through him that we shall be led into the truth in its fullness. There is still mystery, but it is not the mystery of an empty infinity of space and time. It is the mystery of the incarnation and the cross, of the holiness that can embrace the sinner, of a Lord who is servant, and of the deathless one who can die. There is still the vast ocean of what we do not know and do not understand. But we know the way, and the way is Jesus. In the words of Dietrich Bonhoeffer that stand at the head of this essay, "Jesus Christ alone is the certainty of faith." To look for certainty elsewhere is to head for the wasteland.

Both faith and doubt have their proper roles in the whole enterprise of knowing, but faith is primary and doubt is secondary because rational doubt depends upon beliefs that sustain our doubt. The ideal that modernity, following Descrates, has set before itself, namely, the ideal of a kind of certainty that admits no possibility of doubt, is leading us into skepticism and nihilism. The universe is not provided with a spectator's gallery in which we can survey the total scene without being personally involved. True knowledge of reality is available only to the one who is personally committed to the truth already grasped. Knowing cannot be severed from living and acting, for we cannot know the truth unless we seek it with love and unless our love commits us to action. Faith is the only certainty because faith involves personal commitment. The point has often been made that there is a distinction between the cognitive and the affective elements in belief, between "I believe that . . ." and "I believe in. . . ." But faith holds both together; to separate them is to deny oneself access to truth.

The confidence proper to a Christian is not the confidence of one who claims possession of demonstrable and indubitable knowledge. It is the confidence of one who had heard and answered the call that comes from the God through whom and for whom all things were made: "Follow me."

Counseling

- Obligation: - What is right - wrong
  - Permanent moral obligation
  - Tempory ~~tempory~~ tempory moral obligation
  - Christian liberty

- Value -

- Motivation. → (Gratitude to God.)

Construct for Biblical Counseling.

Developing Motivation to be obedient to God.
- Who is God?
- Who am I.?
  - What is sin?
  - What is penalty of sin?

  - What has God done?

My Response?

_____

How do I interpret situation back to the 10" & to Creation Mandate?

Shema -

The Ten.

Counseling

MOVE FROM ————→	TO
CERTAINTY BASED ——→	Certainty BASED on
Human Logic - wisdom	Fidelity of God.
Results Skepticism - Nihilism	Hope.